Gay Old Girls

Gay Old Girls

by Zsa Zsa Gershick

alyson
books

LOS ANGELES • NEW YORK

MANUFACTURED IN THE UNITED STATES OF AMERICA.
PRINTED ON ACID-FREE PAPER.

THIS TRADE PAPERBACK ORIGINAL IS PUBLISHED BY ALYSON PUBLICATIONS INC.,
P.O. BOX 4371, LOS ANGELES, CALIFORNIA 90078-4371.
DISTRIBUTION IN THE UNITED KINGDOM BY TURNAROUND PUBLISHER SERVICES LTD.,
UNIT 3 OLYMPIA TRADING ESTATE, COBURG ROAD, WOOD GREEN,
LONDON N22 6TZ ENGLAND.

FIRST EDITION: NOVEMBER 1998

02 01 00 99 98   10 9 8 7 6 5 4 3 2 1

ISBN 1-55583-476-0

LIBRARY OF CONGRESS CATALOGING-IN-PUBLICATION DATA
GAY OLD GIRLS / BY ZSA ZSA GERSHICK.—1ST ED.
ISBN 1-55583-476-0
1. AGED LESBIANS—UNITED STATES—INTERVIEWS. I. GERSHICK, ZSA ZSA.
HQ75.6.U5G39 1998
305.26—DC21   98-21802 CIP

COVER DESIGN BY B. ZINDA

I will tell you something about stories
They aren't just entertainment
Don't be fooled
They are all we have.
—Leslie Marmon Silko

Contents

Acknowledgments

No book is ever written without considerable assistance, encouragement, and support, but my special thanks go to Noel Riley Fitch, Monika Kehoe, Peggy Albrecht, Delphine DeMore, and Jeanne Gershick: tough, funny, fine women who have helped me to see.

Introduction

When I was 16 years old and suspecting that I might be bisexual, if not outright gay, I sent away for a copy of Dr. David Reuben's vaunted sex manual *Everything You Always Wanted to Know about Sex but Were Afraid to Ask*. It was 1975, the tail end of the Free Love era, and there was almost nothing as shameful as a virgin, someone who hadn't done it in the backseat of her boyfriend's—or girlfriend's—Buick. Although I could have easily purchased a copy at a nearby bookstore, I was too embarrassed to do so. I was hungry for information. Were other women aroused by women as I was? What did they look like? How could I meet them? Had we always existed, hidden from the mainstream? Or were we present in the mainstream, passing because "pretty" women were not what others expected?

Weeks later when the paperback arrived, I waited until late that night to rip away the plain brown wrapper. I turned immediately to the scant and dismissive three-page section on lesbians and was disappointed to discover that, by Dr. Reuben's knowledgeable anatomical standards, I wasn't one at all:

> Occasionally a woman [who is a lesbian] may have an unusually large clitoris which reaches as much as two or more inches in length when erect…What would be a disgrace to a man is a delight to a woman. Lesbians with this anatomical quirk are in great demand.

But I was also relieved, for lesbian relationships, said Reuben, were "stormy" and deceitful. He concluded:

> Basically, all homosexuals are alike—looking for love where there can be no love and looking for sexual satisfaction where there can be no lasting satisfaction.

As laughable as Reuben's misinformation about lesbians is today, this was the best information available to a teenager living in Alameda, Calif., a midsize city situated only a stone's throw from San Francisco. Although The City, a gay mecca since World War II, sat just 20 minutes away by car, I had no contact with its gay bars, bookstores, or neighborhoods. It was 1975, and I was ignorant not only of our lesbian present but also of our lesbian past.

Gay Old Girls is about that lesbian past.

As a reporter for numerous gay and mainstream newspapers and magazines during the 1980s, I often wondered how my lesbian foremothers survived the hostility and invisibility of previous decades. If I could barely find another lesbian, let alone *accurate* information about our relationships and our communities in the mid-1970s—after Stonewall, Gloria Steinem, and the rise and fall of Flower Power—how did women find each other during earlier, darker decades? What were our lives like during the Great Depression, World War II, the McCarthy era, and the Summer of Love? How did we survive and even thrive in a world that told us we were demented and deviant?

In these pages you'll find the stories of some of our lives. You'll meet Jane Stevenson, by all appearances a typical, attractive, postwar American housewife, who—safely ensconced in a split-level suburban home—baked cookies, attended PTA meetings, and made a warm and loving life for her brood, with one important difference: She had a husband *and* a wife. And Valerie Taylor (née Velma Tate), a midwestern schoolteacher who left an abusive husband and headed for Chicago in the 1950s, where she eked out a living writing drugstore romance novels and pulp lesbian fiction, the only woman on an editorial assembly line populated by cigar-smoking men with pen names such as Sylvia Sharon. The torrid pulps—featuring pouty vixens in tight angora sweaters who got the girl, lost the girl, and then killed themselves—proved to Taylor that she could write better books and paved the way for her groundbreaking novels of the 1960s—works in which lesbians didn't kill themselves. These are just two of the women whose stories appear in *Gay Old Girls.*

In 1985 Dr. Monika Kehoe—professor, activist, athlete, and author—urged me to interview older lesbians and record their stories before mortality had its way and their recollections were lost forever. I'd first interviewed Kehoe in connection with a story about her groundbreaking study *Lesbians Over Sixty Speak for Themselves.* In this survey, which later was published in book form, Kehoe and a graduate student associate had created a questionnaire that asked about the sexual, social, religious, family, and work lives of lesbians over 60. Distributing these questionnaires through gay and lesbian bookstores, agencies, and publications, they fielded 100 anonymous responses yielding a wealth of information. It was Kehoe who encouraged me to find these hidden women and flesh out their necessarily terse written responses with face-to-face interviews.

The women whose stories appear in this book are pioneers. Ranging in age from 60 to 80, they do not represent the entirety of the lesbian community, just a small sampling of it. Some were openly gay from adolescence; others married and raised children, coming out only after their sons and daughters had left home or graduated from college. According to Kinsey in his earthshaking *Sexual Behavior in the Human Female,* 8% of the American distaff population is probably gay. Using 1990 Census figures, this means that there are more than two million lesbians over the age of 60 in the United States. How much fuller this portrait might have been if more felt comfortable in coming out. Unfortunately, the majority of these women are still deeply closeted, fearful of what may happen if the truth of their lives is known.

The experience of interviewing these women, now in their later years, has been very much like sitting at an elder family member's knee: In terms of shared experience, they are our great-grand-mothers, grandmothers, and mothers. In these stories we get a glimpse of gay life and longing as it was in such places and periods as Chicago in the '30s, New York in the '40s, Los Angeles in the '50s, and San Francisco in the '60s. It has been my great privilege to listen to these accounts. Upon reading them, I hope that you laugh and cry and, most importantly, remember.

Zsa Zsa Gershick
Los Angeles, 1997

Jane Stevenson
South San Francisco, California

Following Jane Stevenson's directions, I take the South City exit off 101 South and drive along a boulevard that runs parallel to the freeway for a few miles. Then I turn off the large, four-lane thoroughfare onto a quiet residential street and begin my climb up through a hilly suburban settlement of split-level 1950s homes. It is a Saturday, and children are playing in their front yards while young men in ball caps wash and work on their cars or water neatly cut lawns. There are no broken Thunderbird bottles or bums sprawled out on the sidewalks. There are no traffic jams, no blaring horns as there are in my inner-city neighborhood. Except for an occasional plane passing overhead, it is quiet.

In one of these houses lives a woman who was once—by all appearances—a typical, attractive, postwar American housewife. She baked cookies, attended PTA meetings and made a warm and loving life for her brood, with one important difference: She had a husband and a wife.

Jane, 65, is a soft-spoken woman. She is reflective, emotional, unrehearsed. As she talks, some of what she recalls makes her cry.

She shows me photographs of Grace, her partner of nearly 20 years. Grace is good-looking, with strong, Katharine Hepburn cheekbones and a daring expression in her eyes.

Jane also shows me photographs of her husband. In the first one, George "Steve" Stevenson appears in his dress police uniform. He is all

*boot polish and starched blues—a strapping, macho male. Jane hands
me another photo of Steve as he looked at home: He's wearing a white
knit skirt and a top, with a big, red bow perched atop a light-brown
pageboy wig.*

*These three—along with Jane and Steve's son, Mike—lived together
in an extended family that was far more '90s than '50s. They were
avant-garde. To the public, their neighbors, and the guys on the force,
they were the perfect American family, just like Ward, June, Wally, and
the Beav. They read together, ate together, shared a home and their lives
together. Most importantly, they supported, protected, and loved each
other. They were, indeed, the perfect American family—with just a little
twist. Or, as Stevenson describes it, "a life within a life."*

Interviewed November 1986

Jane, Steve, and Grace Settle
Down in Suburbia

J: Grace and I picked out the house. Steve didn't even see it. He
said, "You two go pick out the house." Grace's mother was retiring from her job in Kansas City, and Grace said, "Oh, my God,
my mother's retiring, and she wants to come out and live with us.
What am I going to do?" And I said, "Don't worry; if love is big
enough for four of us, love is big enough for five. Let's just ex-
pand a little and see what happens." And Grace's mother came
out. That's when we bought the house—so we'd have room for
everybody. And that's when the boys went downstairs. [*Laughs*]
Grace and I had the bedroom upstairs, and we had a bedroom
for her mother across the hall. Steve and our son, Mike, went
downstairs. We did this in the other house too. She and I had our
bedroom upstairs and Steve and Mike had their bedrooms downstairs. It was the best we could do.

I think it's very inventive.

J: We said we were avant-garde. We said the world wasn't modern enough to understand us. And that's what we told this little kid growing up. And you know, he accepted it. We didn't give him too much explanation; we just told him that's the way it was in our house. We said our house is different because we were smarter than other people. If he didn't think we were so smart, we'd say look at your dad who's so brilliant, look at your Aunt Grace who's so brilliant, and that's why we're above the others. Isn't that snobbish?

You were advanced.

J: It was. Mike, my son, is now a forest ranger with the National Park Service. He wouldn't have been that, but his father took him out. He and his father went out in the woods camping together. They had a beautiful life together, a life a little city boy wouldn't usually see. They were close. When Steve, my husband, had to travel, he didn't have to worry about my being alone because I always had Grace. Grace wanted a child but knew there'd be no child for her. Mike was her child. It was all built-in for us.

And Steve never had to worry about pleasing you [sexually]?

J: None of that sex crap had to get in the way of our loving each other. When Grace died, no one could have stood by me and been more wonderful than Steve Stevenson. There was no one I could turn to but him. He understood and knew. I could talk to him about it and pour out my anger and my love, and he listened to it and understood. And I understood him because he was sitting there in a dress. [*Laughs*] I knew that he had his need. But we just didn't let all this muck get in the way of it. There are different kinds of love.

Loving families don't have to follow that 1950s nuclear model.

J: I found that out way later. You don't know how relieved I was the first time I heard people say this. It was as if someone had taken a big weight off my back. I was taking a class at San Francisco State, in the women's studies program, and I was talking to one of the gay women, and she spoke of her husband. We began to talk. She told me that she was married and that her husband protected her. I tried to act so nonchalant about it, but inside I was shaking. We didn't know what else to do then. When Grace and I first fell in love, we kept it a secret. I was a happy housewife with a little boy. That was November 1946. When I realized that what was happening to us was a sexual relationship, it was the beginning of 1947. We always celebrated February 3, 1947, as our anniversary.

How did you meet?

J: Well, I consulted with her professionally. I had had a miscarriage and was continuing to bleed horrendously. My gynecologist couldn't find anything wrong, and so he referred me to Grace. She was a gynecologist and also a psychiatrist and brand new to the city. During my visit, we were talking and she told me that she had a new apartment and new furniture coming, and she said, "Do you suppose you could help me?" And I said yes, that I'd be happy to. And she said, "If I gave you the key to my apartment, would you stay there until the furniture comes? You could come by my office on the days when parts of my furniture arrive, and then you could go to my apartment, wait till the furniture comes, and I'll tell you what to do." And so I did. When the rugs came, I told the men where to lay the rugs and so on.

She must have trusted you immediately.

J: Yeah, well, my gynecologist must have told her that I was a very nice person. Then one day her cherry-wood furniture came. She kept telling me that she [*sighs*] ordered solid cherry-wood furniture! Tons of it, coming from Sloans! It's magnificent. And she said that when it comes, she wants the bed here, the dresser here, the double dresser here, and the deacon's bench there, and I want this, that, and the other thing. And I said, "OK, I'll have it ready for you." So, I called her at the office, and I said that the furniture's all in, and I had even made the bed up for her because I knew what she wanted. Boy, I really did it. I put the sheets on the bed, and I put the bedspread on, and I did the whole thing. And I called her, and I said, "Oh, you come home! Everything's here, your bedroom furniture and everything. It's all gorgeous!" She said, "I'm coming home as soon as I can!" So, she came home and walked into the bedroom, and she looked at it and said, "Isn't it beautiful, isn't it beautiful!" She lay down on the bed, and she said, "Oh, it's just what I dreamed of; it's just what I've wanted." And then she said, "Come here." I walked over to the side of the bed and looked down at her. And she said, "No, I mean come *here*." And she pulled me down on her bed and began to make love to me. [*Sighs*]

That's pretty inspiring furniture.

J: I'm still sleeping on it!

The whole episode was quite daring.

J: It was daring of her, wasn't it? She had been a lesbian before.

And you?

J: I don't really know. There was just something there, but I didn't know from...I mean, there was only housewives loving their husbands and having little boys with runny noses. [*Laughs*] That's all there was in life. I know another thing that attracted us to one another. When I came to see her in her office, I had Albert Camus' *The Myth of Sisyphus*. And she said, "Are you reading that?" And I said, "Yes." And she said, "That's a series of essays." And I said, "So what?" She said, "You know who Sisyphus is?" I said, "Yes—yes, ma'am." And she started to talk to me about Albert Camus while she was examining me. When she said good-bye she told me she didn't know anybody in town except this one doctor. She needed help, and she also said that it was wonderful to meet somebody who doesn't just talk about medicine, golf, and sex. She said just come by the office and get the key and thank you very much for helping me. She loved books. She had a "great books" collection. She sat down with me over a period of years and made me read all the books. Not *made* me read them—we read them together. What I didn't understand, she helped me to understand. I can't explain it all. We were just two people who loved each other.

Now. But what about when all this began?

J: It was turmoil! I'd be making love to her, and I'd say to myself, "I'm making love with a woman!" She'd schedule her cases so that we could go to her house to make love, and then I'd go home in time to make dinner for my husband and child. [*Laughs*] She arranged for a baby-sitter for my child. [*Laughs*] She arranged everything. Very smooth. But I was in turmoil because I thought, "My God, what am I doing?" For two years all this went on, this sneaking around. Then she dropped the big thing in my lap. She said, "I'm going to give up my apartment in San Francisco. I'm going to Mill Valley." She said, "I would go to Sausalito, but there are too many lesbians there." She told me that if you move to Sausalito, they think you're a lesbian. [*Laughs*] She said, "I found a wonderful apartment where I can see my patients, and there's a swimming pool if you want to come over and swim. There's a place for you if you want to come over and be with me forever."

What did you do?

J: I didn't know what to do. I was sick! I said, "What about my child?" She said, "That's the way it is; I'm a psychiatrist first. This is what I do for a living. Come and see me." I said, "I'll leave everybody." She said, "We just can't go on like this behind Steve's back. He's so friendly and nice. I go over and have dinner with all of you, and I love Mike. Everybody's friendly, and here I am making love to you! I have to get out of here!" So I went to Steve that night as he was sitting on the bed taking off his shoes, and I stood by him, and I said, "Steve, there's something I have to tell you that's going to cause us a divorce." He just looked up at me and said, "You mean about you and Grace?" And I said, "You know?" He said, "I've always known; it's very obvious! I didn't know how to tell you because I didn't want to frighten either one of you. So, let's sit down and figure this out. You want to leave me and leave your child? I'll fight for the child. Grace loves Mike very much. I get along with Grace and love her very much as a friend. She's like a sister to me. You love Grace. Why not continue the relationship? Why doesn't Grace move in with us? Just ask her and see what happens!"

Well, the movers were already packing Grace up to go to Mill Valley when I told her this. She stopped the movers, and we had a conference. She cried and said, "Oh, Jane, this would be a dream come true! I'll keep the place in Mill Valley as an office, but I'll live here with your permission." Then she added, "But what will happen? The world isn't ready for us." She knew by this time that Steve wore dresses.

And you knew it also.

J: Oh, yes. I'd known it from the beginning. I knew it on the night we were married.

Was it a surprise?

J: Yes, it was a great surprise. [*Laughs*] I had a beautiful blue peignoir, and I was combing my hair, and he was dressing in the dressing room. He walked out of the dressing room in a white embroidered peignoir. It was prettier than mine. [*Laughs*] I'd been upstaged on my wedding night.

What did you do?

J: I went up to him and put my arms around him. He didn't say anything; he just looked at me imploringly, like "please understand me." I put my arms around him, and I said, "I love you." He said, "I can't help this." I said, "You don't have to explain. I love you. Tonight you don't have to explain. I accept it." I didn't know what it was. I was too young and too stupid to know, I guess. Thank God.

Had you any suspicions beforehand?

J: Yes, I had. He was very interested in women's clothes and in whatever I wore. Whatever he picked out for me to wear, my boss would say, "*That* is really good-looking, Miss Preston!" And I would remember that Steve had picked it out. So, Grace moved in with us, and she had her office in Mill Valley. She lived in South San Francisco with us, but all her mail went to Mill Valley. Even we were scared to death of what we were doing. It was like stepping off into the dark. But we didn't know what else to do. If there had been a divorce, there would have been a scandal. People would ask, "Why is there a divorce between you two people who love each other so dearly? Why a grabbing of the child?"

There could have been the accusation, "My wife is a lesbian." I could have said, "My husband is a transvestite." Of course, I didn't know the word then. I suppose he knew the word "lesbian." I have no idea. Neither words were ever used, but it could have been a very nasty, rotten divorce. Listen, he was relieved. The whole statement of Grace's moving in was my saying, "You don't have to do your husbandly duties toward me or anything. I don't expect anything from you except your friendship and your protection." It was a relief for him because he couldn't have cared less about sex. He was into his philosophical research society and his Boy Scout activities with Mike. When our other little boy died, he started to take Mike out camping in the woods. And Steve and Grace liked Western movies, and I didn't like them. So, when he'd come home and say, "Anyone wanna go to a Western tonight?" Grace would say, "I've had it with people today. Take me." And off they'd go.

And the thing is that people are so stupid—they're so heterosexually minded—that rumors about Steve and Grace being involved flew. People wondered, "How could I let another woman move into the house and go out with my husband? Didn't I realize the dangers of this?" [*Laughs*] But by that time we all had our feet planted firmly in our love and our feelings for each other. We knew where we were in this situation. So I'd come home and I'd say, "You know what I heard today? That lady across the street says that you're being unfaithful to me." Or I'd say to Grace, "The lady next door is saying that you're going to steal my husband." Grace'd sit by the living room window, and she'd put her arm around me, and she'd kiss me and say, "See, they're all thinking I'm going to steal your husband, so it's all right to kiss you in front of everybody." Nobody ever noticed.

Listen, when her mother moved in that was another funny thing. I remember we were making a fire in the fireplace, and her mother came over and put her arm around me and said, "Jane, you don't know how much I appreciate the sacrifice you and

Steve are making for my daughter." [*Laughs*] She said, "Mr. Stevenson lets you sleep upstairs with poor, dear Grace, who's so tired. He lets you take such good care of her." And I said, "Gee, thank you, Mrs. Richmond." She thanked us and never guessed. She didn't live with us for very long. It was too far away from the city. So she got a job in the city almost immediately. We drove her in, and we settled her there. She'd come down once in a while, but she never stayed for more than two or three hours, and then she'd leave. She couldn't stand it out here.

How long did you all live together?

J: Eighteen years. And someplace during the end of it, Grace had cancer. She had cancer before she told us about it. She gave a little hint. Now I can see. She opened up an office in Hawaii in '60 or '61. She had me come over there. I flew over and visited her twice. We burned up the wires phoning between here and Hawaii. Then she came back again. When she came back I hardly recognized her: she was very thin. She was very sick. It just didn't work, whatever happened in Hawaii didn't work. I guess she was looking for some way to get well. I don't know what she was doing, grasping at straws? I remember her saying, "I wish it was just the two of us. I wish you could just leave Steve and come with me, stay with me." I said, "I can't." She said, "Well, I have to be with you." When she resettled here she said, "I don't want you to have to take care of me." She stopped working, closed her office. The reason she closed her office was that son of a bitch—the man who was her colleague and shared the office. All those years everything was OK. Well, after she moved down here, he began to get suspicious that something was not all right. And he started giving out little digs. And finally he said to her, "I think it's better if we don't have an office together, but I've been here longer, so you'd better move out." That's when she went to Hawaii. That's right—that's when she went to Hawaii. She was really broken up about it. She told me, "I think John knows; he's being very nasty about this." So when she came back from Hawaii, she didn't practice anymore. We just played for the rest of the time. We took our books and went to Skyline Park. We'd sit and read together in the sunshine. We drove around and had a lovely time. She did all the driving; I didn't drive. Nobody would let me learn to drive. That wasn't my role. Talk about stereotypes! I was a mama, I suppose. I was the nurturer.

You were everybody's wife!

J: Yes. I was the wife of the husband, the wife of the wife, the mother of the kid. Only one of the mothers of the kid because if there was any trouble or he would say I want something and we'd say no, he would go to his Aunt Grace. And if he asked his Aunt Grace, nine times out of ten she'd say, "Of course, here's a check!" [*Laughs*] It's like that picture in which he's wearing that leather jacket and leaning against his Aunt Grace. In fact, even now—I can't do it now because I can't walk—he used to send money and say please put flowers on his Aunt Grace's grave. I'd tell him, "That's an unnecessary act." And he'd say, "You don't have to do it; she's my Aunt Grace." And he'd go and do it. He loved her very much. Very, very much. In fact, when [my former roommate] Monika came to live here, he didn't realize that Monika was just my friend. I remember he went into the kitchen, and he said, "My Aunt Grace was a lady! What is that dyke doing in your living room?"

What did you say?

J: I told him to shut up, that it was none of his business! I was terribly embarrassed. You can see where the kitchen is and where we are. You can hear everything. So I came into the living room, and I said, "I apologize for what my son has just said, Monika."

She said, "He's just worried because he thinks I'm a threat. He's just thinking about his Aunt Grace. He doesn't realize that I'm just a friend." She is very, very wise. So that's it in a capsule.

When you and Grace were together, did you ever venture into a gay bar?

J: I never knew there were gay establishments. I'm sure she didn't either. I went with her to many medical conferences, and we'd go out to dinner and first have a cocktail at a cocktail lounge together sometimes, but we never went to anything gay. I had no contact with the gay world. Never, until after my husband died. Until after I went to school. At school I took a course in lesbian literature. Got real brave. I mean, I was really brave to do that because I'd dove into the closet and slammed the door. I thought that was it. My lesbian life ended when Grace died. I didn't think of it as a lesbian life either.

What did you think of it as?

J: Two people who love each other. An extended family. I was trying to think if I'd ever heard the word "lesbian." When Grace was in Hawaii, she said to me, "Boy did I have a scrape! I have a patient who thinks she's in love with me—she's a lesbian. [*Laughs*] I don't know how she did it, but she got hold of my telephone number, and she called me at 1 o'clock." I said, "You tell her to get away from you!" [*Laughs*] That's the only time I'd heard that word. We kind of looked down on lesbians. There was a place called Mona's on Broadway. I never went near it with her, and I don't know if she ever went there. I went there with my husband one time. We went there by mistake. We were taking people from out of town through the nightclubs, and we went into Mona's. I remember sitting there, and they were all women, and they were acting in the most bizarre manner. I had a feeling that I had some connection with these people, and yet, I kept thinking that these people were unreal. There was something inside me. Then my husband said, "Let's get out of here; this is a weirdo joint."

What did you see there?

J: I remember there were women in tuxedos. That's all I remember. And I remember two or three times we were in the Black Cat. And I remember sitting down with a naval officer's wife. She and I were sitting there, and our husbands were in the bathroom. And some woman came up and asked me if I'd like to dance. I didn't look like this then. I was quite slender and quite attractive and very feminine with a swishy hairdo and the whole bit. And she asked me to dance, and I said, "No, thank you." And she said, "Do you think you're too good for people like me?" I said, "No, I don't. It's just that I'm waiting for my husband." When I said that, she just said "excuse me" and walked away. That was it. I said something in my own defense to the other woman, but inside my head, all I could think of, something inside of me said, *You're connected to all of this.* And I also thought, *You're leaning on Steve again. You're leaning on Steve to protect you.* Something inside me wanted to get up and say, "Yes, I'd love to dance!" Of course, I was sitting there as Mrs. Stevenson, and there was no way. What can I say? There's such a thin line between the conscious and the subconscious. Consciously, of course, I would say, "No, thank you." But something inside, the same thing I felt at Mona's, connected here. "This is where I belong. I belong here." I wanted to go back, and we did go back with somebody else, but Steve didn't want to. He said, "I don't like to go there, Jane. That's not a savory place, really." I said, "It's exciting, though!" [*Laughs*] I went back two or three times. This was the '50s. Never by myself. Mona's and the Black Cat were there for quite a while, and I could have gone into Mona's more than once. I'll bet you anything I dragged Steve into Mona's more than once. I remember being in Mona's, and I remember the woman in the tuxedo outside asking people to come in. She was a barker. I was never there with Grace. I can't see Grace in that type of situation at all.

You never did mention what happened to Grace.

J: One day, the idea and the reality of wasting away from cancer was just too much for Grace, and she took a handgun and drove up to Skyline Boulevard, and she shot herself right through the heart. As a doctor, she knew right where to aim. Death was instantaneous. That night when she didn't come home, something in me knew. And then the telephone call came. It was shocking. I wish she hadn't done it. I loved her so much; it would have been my pleasure to have taken care of her until the end. But she had so much pride. She didn't want me to watch her decline. I've had two or three relationships since Grace, but they haven't lasted. I loved her more than I can even say.

Is it difficult for you now to be in large groups of lesbians?

J: I'm uncomfortable, and I hate myself for it. I don't know what to say. I went to a dance one time, and a lady asked me, "What kind of work do you do?" I said, "I'm a housewife." She said, "Oh, you were married?" I said, "Yes." She said, "When did you divorce your husband?" I said, "Never." She just looked at me and didn't know what else to ask. I sat quietly alone for the rest of the dance. [*Laughs*] I want to be part of it, but I don't feel part of it.

Margaret Kennedy
San Francisco, California

*"Even though I'm out of the closet, I still live in one," says Margaret
Kennedy, 74, welcoming me with humor into her tiny studio apartment in the Tenderloin. Her posture is perfect, her hands are strong and
square, and her gestures are decisive as she points out the decorative
highlights: poster portraits of Albert Einstein and Imogene Cunning-
ham, NASA photos of Mars taken by Voyager during its first mission.*

*Margaret's penny loafers are shined to a high gloss, and her navy
blue corduroy slacks are neatly pressed. Her white tuxedo shirt is
starched but soft from frequent launderings, and her hair is white and
close-cropped like an athlete's. She wears horn-rimmed preppy glasses
that give her a decidedly academic appearance.*

*In the last year she has undergone triple bypass surgery; in the next
two years, after 50 years of smoking, she will have a lung removed,
and the vitality she is known for will have evaporated. But on the day
of this interview she is vibrant, often taking the floor during our discussion to physically illustrate the activities and events of seven decades.*

*"I can't show you pictures of myself as a child or as a younger adult
because about six years ago, after a visit with my sister on the East
Coast, I came back to San Francisco and destroyed every symbol of our
past lives altogether," she says wistfully. "I think it was a symbolic mur-
der. I've rather regretted that—I should have at least saved a few pictures of me."*

Indeed. Those pictures would have illustrated her tea-smoking days, running with her "gang of gals" at the University of Chicago in the early 1930s; her service as a WAC in the Pacific during the allied invasion of the Philippines; her 22 years as a stewardess aboard a Norwegian cargo vessel traveling around the globe; and her tours of duty aboard a towboat traversing the Mississippi and Missouri rivers— among many other adventures.

"My sister and I are the antithesis of each other, and our chemistry never did mesh," says Margaret. "The fighting started between us as very small children, and we still have a very tempestuous relationship. I think we began fighting in the womb."

Margaret is an atheist, a secular humanist, a fellow traveler, a rover. She is a realist in every regard.

"I'm old. I admit that at this age I'm pretty much at the end of the line," she says. "My sister says to me, 'It's too bad that when you were younger you couldn't have taken care of things for your old age. You could have gotten a husband.' And I said, 'Listen, many women get married and have nothing at the end of their lives.' Children grow up and desert parents. I mean, they give them lip service and call under protest at Christmas or Thanksgiving. I've led the life I wanted, and I'm at peace with it."

Interviewed February 1986

You Are Not Alone: Remembrances of a Lesbian WAC

M: About a year ago I underwent triple bypass surgery on my heart. That's where they take the veins out of your legs and they put them here in the chest. One of the things I recently told an audience is that since I've had the surgery I no longer have any sexual feeling, and I miss that. Well, they just gasped! Later on, after the whole thing broke up, a couple of RNs came over to me.

One was a female, one was a male, and they said it's probably the medication. Once you stop that, then everything will be back to normal. Of course, I'm stuck with the medication for the rest of my life. I have my own little pharmacopoeia over here [points to a table with five or six pill bottles on it] that I have to take for one thing or another. So, as a consequence, I'm sexless. I don't even dream about it anymore. Until that thing happened to me, I had very strong erotic feelings for women. Now, I still adore women, but the eroticism is gone.

Just two weeks ago I saw my cardiologist. I asked him about the lack of erotic feeling of any sort. He said, "Listen, Miss Kennedy, we saved your life! Look at you today; you nearly died." I said, "Yes, I'm aware of that." "Well, we can't give you everything," he said. Which is true, of course. [*Laughs*]

Well, anyway, I was born in 1911 in the deep, deep South in a tiny backwater town called Fulton, Alabama. It's no longer on the map, by the way; it has disappeared. I was taken as a very young infant to live in Selma. Selma at that time had a population of about 25,000 people. And I lived in a world of black faces because half the population was black. It was almost 100% Baptist, except for a few Methodists in the town. My parents belonged to the Methodist Church, and that was the first religion to which I was exposed.

We attended the public schools there, my twin sister, my brother and I. And when I was about 11, we moved to Montgomery, Alabama. That's another very Southern city, which at that time had a population of about 6,000. I had two years of college at a little place that Sinclair Lewis described in his book *Ann Vickers* as the type of college that doesn't quite meet the standards of a first-class public high school.

My twin sister, by the way, is not a lesbian. She is the most homophobic. [*Laughs*] We're not identicals. We're fraternals and two very different women altogether. She is such an absolutely proper and painfully correct person. Terribly.

I remember years ago when I was still living in the closet, trying to be a heterosexual for the outer world and always to my sister, of course, a heterosexual. I had a date with a man in New York City, and she came into the city to visit me. I introduced her to this man, and she said, "By the way, where did you meet this man?"

Well, I knew the way she felt was that men and women are introduced to each other formally, you know: "Miss Smith, this is Mr. Jones…" I lived a completely different life. So I turned to her and said, "I picked him up on the Fifth Avenue bus! That was three years ago, and we're still seeing each other!" [*Laughs*]

She sounds very much like the stereotypical Southern belle.

M: Oh, yes, very much. I thought she was destined to be an old maid.

How did you discover that you were gay?

M: At the age of 19 I ran away from home. Well, I had run away from home three times before that, and each time I came back, my mother, who was a very severe woman—that was another tempestuous relationship, we didn't get along from day one—said, if you leave this house once more, you'll never set foot across that threshold again!" Well, at the age of 19 I did leave and I never went back except to visit.

Where did you go?

M: Well, I went to Chicago, where I enrolled in business school. My father felt very sympathetic toward me because our mother was just impossible to live with. He financed my living in Chicago to attend this very luxurious business academy. That's where you went to school from 9 in the morning to 3 in the afternoon— five days a week, you know—just to turn out a first-class secretary. [*Laughs*] The training was marvelous in every way, and it became helpful to me in later years.

So, I studied in Chicago and received this stipend from home. But also when I was in Chicago, I discovered the lesbian world. And the University of Chicago became my camping grounds because I ran into a whole slew of boys and girls who belonged to the gay world there. But it was such an isolated, close-knit little community, you know, and all of us were living in the closet. Definitely so. Around town I discovered where the several lesbian hangouts were. And my studies at the academy, which were supposed to last for two years, began to decline because I was too active in that other world.

Furthermore, I had begun to smoke pot. I was about 20 [in 1931], and I didn't know anything about pot, but I picked it up at the University of Chicago. I didn't really think of pot outside of that, but I used to run with those boys and girls and they smoked pot. We didn't call it pot, though; we called it *tea*, t-e-a, because if you looked at this stuff, it looked like green tea. I still remember that you got two of them [joints] for 25 cents, and it was not against the law. Two joints for 25 cents! It became against the law in 1937 with the Marijuana Tax Act. But we had no trouble whatever buying it, although it wasn't done that openly.

On Friday nights at the University of Chicago we'd say, "Let's go out and get some tea!" So the hat would be passed amongst the girls, and it was only two for a quarter, and when we had a whole collection of quarters, we'd get into the girls' automobiles and go down to the Negro neighborhood on the north side. And one of the girls would get out and go up to this old shamble of a house, knock on the door, and she'd pass the money in and come out with a whole load of tea. And we would spend the weekend—Friday night, Saturday night, and Sunday afternoon—smoking pot, smoking tea.

I began to have some very frightening reactions. What you call a bad trip. Using the stuff frightened me several times. For instance, one time I was with the others and I had the impression that my body was separated from my head. My head was floating up in space all alone, and my body was down here. I began to say, "Where's my body, where's my body," and I couldn't feel it. It was terribly frightening. I became hysterical. Gad, they had to take me home and stay overnight with me. They said, "You just had a bad trip." Well, I was afraid of the stuff after that, and I didn't use it for a long time.

And then I used it again. And that time I was on the third floor of an old building on the south side of Chicago with my gang of gals, and the window was open. It was night outside, darkness, and we were in this well-lighted room with the windows standing wide open because we didn't want the rest of the people in the building to smell the tea. We wanted to keep it ventilated, you know. And I kept looking out this window, thinking to myself, *I think I'll go out that window and see if I can actually fly to the ground.* You can get killed that way, you know. And I became alarmed because I thought I was going to do it. The impulse was overpowering. That frightened me very much.

Did that end your tea-smoking days?

M: No. I talked to a social worker there in the city. I told her that I had been smoking tea with the other girls. She slapped me and said, "I'm sending you to see Dr. so-and-so, who's a psychiatrist, and you can have a talk with him!" So I talked with him, and he said, "Well, stay away from these people. That's bad business you've become entangled in." "But," I said, "they're my friends." When you're a young woman in a big city like Chicago, you value your friends. Furthermore, they were doing all of the things in the lesbian world that I wanted to do. The only thing I could do was give them up.

By that time I had become acquainted with lesbians who did not use tea. I met a newspaperwoman who was quite a prominent person there in Chicago. She worked for the Hearst newspaper, and she had a column called Prudence Penny in the women's section of the newspaper, you know. Her name wasn't Prudence Penny, of course—that was just the column's name. I began to run around with her, and she knew everybody in Chicago. She was well-known in the journalistic world, and she was a lesbian.

So, I moved into a different sphere, away from the lesbians I'd smoked tea with and into a world of people who didn't smoke tea. And it was far more interesting. But I don't look back with any anger toward these particular girls who I knew at the time. I liked them. For years I kept snapshots of us. There were the masculine ones and the feminine ones.

When you went to Chicago did you know that you were gay?

M: No, this is an interesting thing. The psychiatrist asked me how long I'd been a homosexual. Well, I had read that word, and I knew the girls I was running with liked each other and everything, but I really came out among these college students. You know, to a knowledge of myself. But then the doctor began to explain quite a few things to me. He finally turned me over to a woman psychiatrist, and she recommended certain books for me to read. I began to read remnants of Sappho's poetry and all that sort of thing. I'd dig it out of the public library. I learned about Gertrude Stein, and of course I read Freud. And I would go twice a week to see her, you see. She educated me about some of the psychological aspects. She also pointed out to me that I wasn't alone. That's one of the things I remember her telling me: "You are not alone. There are many, many women like you." That was 50 years ago. I'm 74, you must remember. We were all in the closet.

I often look at this [gay] life now and [think] that it came too late for me. Because I have tried to live two lives. A dichotomy, you might say. In a certain world I was a homosexual pretending to be a heterosexual woman, and I had sexual relationships with men, for instance, which were all a damn lie. It was something you made yourself do because you had to show the world. It was a front that you deliberately put up to keep this other thing hidden in the closet. And from the time I left Alabama and became acquainted with the lesbians in Chicago—and after that, in every big city I was ever in—I went looking for the lesbian world. But I always had to maintain this closet life on one side and the heterosexual life on the other side—especially in my occupational life. I had any number of jobs. I was a consummate failure as an employee anywhere. I didn't care to stick to one thing for very long.

What were some of the things that you did?

M: Mostly, before the war, I did office work, and in that way the training that I received in Chicago came in very handy for me. I had one job in New York City at the very height of the Depression. I was the one-woman office staff of this very small firm. It was owned and operated by a woman, an old maid, and it was a very fine, expensive book-binding shop. I spent three years there. I used to say to myself, "I'd love to be a writer." I always admired women who were writers and stood in awe of men who were writers. But I said, "Since I can't write books, I'll make them!" So that sort of gave me a place.

I was working there almost until I went into the Army. And then, when I went into the Army I wrote to her from Fort Des Moines, Iowa, where I was undergoing basic training, and she wrote me back this wonderful letter. She said, "I'm so proud of you! I wish that I were as young as you; I too would be in uniform!" Of course, the World War was on, and a lot of women felt like that.

Where did you enlist?

M: I enlisted here, in San Francisco. I came from that job working for her in New York City to San Francisco. And you may say, "Why?" It's because I always wanted to come to the West Coast. That's how free I was to go wherever I wished to go! I came out to the West Coast first with a lesbian that I knew on the East Coast, and we parted company up in Seattle. She was a physiotherapist. She worked in hospitals, you know. She was a marvelous girl, and I enjoyed her. So, we came out here together, but on the way out we decided to look over the West, and we decided to go to Sun Valley, Idaho, a very swank, ski resort. Our money was getting a bit low at the time, and we decided to take jobs as waitresses. So, we became waitresses there in Sun Valley for the whole winter and saved our money because we were going to explore the world.

I remember one of the most famous movie actresses at that time—because Sun Valley was a gathering place for the movie world—was Norma Shearer. She was the reigning queen, you know, and in the dining room she was my guest. I had to serve her table, you know. She was a marvelous woman, and she was there with her three children spending the winter. Ernest Hemingway was there at Sun Valley—not in Sun Valley itself, but the little town in Idaho [Ketchum] where he died. He came to Sun Valley for the food mostly and to drink. He was a heavy drinker. President Roosevelt was in the White House, and he had four sons, you know. And three of them were playboys, and they hit Sun Valley all the time. You saw those people. It was sort of an interesting world to move in, even though your status was not quite high.

But nonetheless, my friend, Betty, and I, we kept our money and saved it very carefully. And then we got to Seattle, Washington. Well, that's where we came to a parting of the ways. She decided to go back East, and I was enchanted by the West Coast. So I came down here to San Francisco. I came to this city not knowing a soul or anything—when you're young, I don't know, you can do anything! So, I walked to the biggest and swankest hotel in the city, the Saint Francis, and got hired as a waitress. That was in 1940.

That's where I was working at the time the Japanese attacked Pearl Harbor. I was earning marvelous money. [*Laughs*] The wages were terrible—it wasn't even unionized in those days. Today it is. But the tips were excellent. I was banking a $100 a week from just tips only.

I couldn't find any lesbians here in San Francisco; I still remember that! In my free time, you know, off the job and everything, I went trying to find my way around the city. And I had a date with a man one night. We went up to Broadway, and he said, "Have you ever been to Finocchio's? I didn't even know anything about Finocchio's. Well, after that I knew. Here were these men working as female impersonators in a stage show in a cabaret. They must know where something's going on in San Francisco! So I went back after that one evening at Finocchio's and got acquainted with some of the boys who were dancing in the chorus line. [*Laughs*] I asked, "Where do the girls go around here?" And one answered, "There's really no place in town for them." Well, in New York I was part of the Greenwich Village scene. In Chicago I'd been part of the north of Rush Street neighborhood where the bohemian world was, you know, but I never did find any place at that time, in 1940, that lesbians frequented here in the city. I don't think there was any place.

But I did meet a girl who was working as a waitress here. She was a very masculine looking girl—very short, mannish type of haircut, you know, and a very masculine gait. I don't know how she got a job with this butch look, but she did, she had a job. She was a waitress somewhere else in the city, and I began to go around with her, but I never did love her or anything. She was sort of a bosom pal—you know, a buddy.

And then World War II came along, and our nation was at war. Here, in San Francisco, the city was under blackout. Everything was just in a fever, you know. And I said to myself, "We are at war; I wonder how I can get into this thing?" You wanted to get into the war, you see, because all over the city people were leaving their jobs in droves to go and work in Oakland. We lost half of the waitress staff at the Saint Francis going over to work in the shipyards, wearing hard hats, you know. [*Laughs*] Rosie the Riveter, that type of thing. All over town it was the same thing—everybody was going to work in the big wartime factories. Down the line here on the Peninsula, the big aircraft factories were going full pace, you know, and a lot of people went to that. I went over and investigated Oakland for the shipyards because I knew two women who worked there. They shared an apartment here in the city, and they'd come home at night from Oakland with their hard hats on just exhausted, black all over, soaked because they were welding ships together! [*Laughs*] I decided it was a little too rough for me. Can you imagine anything being too rough for me? But it was so dirty! Really, it was such a dirty job, and it was noisy. So I stuck to my waitress work.

And one day I was walking down Market Street, and I saw the

very first of the Women's Army Corps posters going up along the sidewalks. You know, "Uncle Sam Needs You!" Well, he was looking for women now. It showed these women in Army uniforms, you know, saluting, and I said, "The Women's Army Corps! The WAC! I wonder if I'd be eligible for that!" [*Laughs*] And I kept thinking it over in my mind, and I talked to people about it and they said, "Yes, but they only get $50 a month." And I said, "Yes, but you're in uniform!" It was an economic factor, to give up what I was earning at the Saint Francis to be in uniform for $50 a month. But I thought, "No, I have to get into this war! And I just actually had to. And I went down to the recruiting office and inquired about it; and just like that, they set me up for an interview, and within 30 days I was in uniform! Oh boy, they grab you! [*Laughs*] We were told to stand by, and I stood by, and I got my "greetings." "Greetings" is a form letter that you get from the Army, and it says "Greetings, you are now a member of the Women's Army Corps, and you will report to such and such a place—it was down at the foot of Market Street—to board a troop train that will take you to your basic training." And I went down there with the clothes I had on my back on that date because that letter told me to be there.

I had a man friend here in the city who was crazy about me— he wanted to marry me. I mean, he was a suitor who was devoted to me. And I often felt, because he didn't know anything about my being a lesbian, it almost seemed unfair, you know. I didn't lead him on or anything of that sort, but he was sure that I was going to marry him. And I've had a couple experiences of that sort with men who expected I was going to marry them, and I didn't. I didn't want to. But, I would never let my hair down and say, "Oh no, I'm a lesbian," or anything of that sort. So I was still living in the closet, you see.

Anyway, this man came down to the foot of Market Street. There was a railroad track along there, and this long troop train was lined up to take both the men and the women from the Bay

Area off to basic training. And there he was. And he gave me this envelope. He said, "You know, when I went through my Army stint, it was hard to get along on $24 a month as a private." That's what he got when he was a private, and I was joining at $50 a month. In this letter he had two $20 bills inside. [*Laughs*] He said, "You'll need this when you get there, I know it." I finally found myself on this crowded train. And we had three long days from San Francisco to Fort Des Moines, Iowa.

And when I got to Des Moines, the first time I ever heard a female sergeant's voice was right there at the railroad station. When we all tumbled out, there were about 85 of us that came from this area right here. This female sergeant—I was sure she was a lesbian. I mean, she looked like a man! She had a short haircut, and she was wearing her uniform. She said, *"OK, fall out!"* [*Laughs*] And that was the beginning. I came to like that gal—as a person, you know—because I knew that she was keeping herself hidden in this female world that we were living in.

The very first thing our sergeant did during the first two weeks we were there, was to march us to this huge auditorium there on the base, and three women officers, lieutenants, got up before us on the stage and spoke through a microphone and said, "Now we're going to give you some of the protocol of being in the Army." And so forth. And then—and this is something that, boy, just ate right into this little ole brain of mine—the lieutenant said: "There's one thing that will not be tolerated in this women's army, and that is an unwholesome, abnormal friendship between two women. If we discover any of these personal relationships going on, the Army will deal with it summarily, and you will not be here long!"

Now, she didn't come out and say "homosexuality" will not be allowed or "lesbianism" will not be allowed, she said "unwholesome friendships." So, we all finally fell out of the auditorium and we were in ranks going back to the barracks—hup, two, three, four—and some of the girls around me, talking out of the sides of their mouths like convicts, said, "What's she mean about that unwholesome, abnormal friendship thing?" I said to one, "You don't know what that means?" "No, no, I don't know what it means." Well, the girl came from a farm somewhere up in Minnesota; why should she know what that meant? But nonetheless, though, that thing just ate into me. And I said, "Uh oh, be careful, you know— be very careful. Don't fall in love with anybody, and don't make any passes whatever!"

At the end of basic training, though, you scatter. People are assigned to different things. I got assigned there at Fort Des Moines to go to the women officers' training area, where I was a supply corporal. Then we received indoctrination courses about going overseas, but we didn't know where we were going. Nobody told us. It didn't occur to us that we'd be in the Pacific because you could have been sent to Europe or some other place.

I was writing all sorts of letters all over the map, by gad. I wrote people saying, "I'm going overseas somewhere. I don't know where it is, but I'll keep in touch." I got in touch with my brother. He was especially unsympathetic toward having a sister who went into uniform in the army. He didn't mind my sister being in the Red Cross. That was a ladylike thing, you know. I remember him telling me, "That's no place for a woman! That's a man's world!" I said, "Well, it's a woman's world now because I'm in it. I'm in uniform." "Jesus," he said, "do you know what soldiers do to women when they catch them alone out in far places?" The thing is, the whole time I was in uniform, until I got out altogether, I never had any sex relationships with any of the men. Some people had the idea that women were very loose with things. But you had discipline. There are all sorts of restrictions. If you did make an ass of yourself by becoming promiscuous or loose in your very personal, private life, you wouldn't be there for very long. They'd get rid of you.

I eventually ended up on a supply vessel in the Philippine Islands. I was at Leyte and also in Manila. I never did like the native Filipinos that I met over there when I was in uniform. I didn't like them at all. They had performed a number of acts of sabotage against us American troops on the island of Leyte—that was the invasion point for the Philippines, you know. It was the Filipinos who did these things; it was not the Japanese. They blew up several of our ships right there. I mean, that's the kind of warfare that I found myself in the midst of. The instructions from the officers were, "Tell your people not to be friendly with the Filipinos. We think that the Filipinos are doing these things to us!" There was no evidence that the Japanese were doing it. What we learned later was that there were Filipinos who didn't want us to come back. See, when General MacArthur left the Philippine Islands he said, "I shall return!" Those immortal words, you know, that he uttered at the time. And he did return—he returned at Leyte. But the Filipinos had always considered themselves to be nothing but a colony of the United States of America, and many of them didn't want us to come back! [*Laughs*] They didn't like us. And here we come back to take their islands away from the Japanese. They thought we'd restore them to colonial status again for another 80 or 90 years, so they carried out acts of sabotage against us. And that was pretty well proven. So, as a consequence, I took a dislike to the Filipinos. When you see a ship blow up right in front of you—maybe 150 yards away, just suddenly explodes like that—because someone has gone underneath and put something against the bulkhead underwater, and it happens again and again and again—it's a terrible thing! Now, we could understand the Japanese planes that would come in and bomb the ships. At least we knew it was coming. But this thing underneath. Because down in the hold of this huge supply ship that I was on, you had 8,000 drums of high octane gasoline that was to be delivered to the Army Air Force. Once the planes would land, they'd need aviation gasoline. And that's what we had down there in this huge ship. On top of that, we had K rations, C rations, field rations, garrison rations, medical supplies. We even had condoms for the troops, you know. They'd give them out free. And stuff of that sort. I was absolutely terrified that a Filipino was going to get down under that ship and those 8,000 drums of high octane gasoline would go up. I had to live on that ship! I didn't want to be blown to pieces by the Filipinos. So I developed this terrible fear—that's the only way I can describe it. It doesn't interfere with your daily work, but there's a sort of dread that you live with inside you that the ship was going to be blown up.

And as it was, the ship was not blown up, but we eventually got a kamikaze plane. Now, when I was in the invasion of Leyte, "kamikaze" was not a word in our vocabulary. We were too new at the Japanese language at that time. We just called them "suicides." The Japanese planes would come in and each pilot of these suicides would assign themselves to this one or that one and pancake themselves right into the ship. I mean, right into the ship! Just like that. I saw it happen to other ships, but we always escaped—until one Sunday morning at about 9 o'clock we got ours. A suicide. It came in and blew off the forward mast of the ship. There were five young crewmen who manned that gun on the bow of the ship. It was a large gun. And the kamikaze blew them to pieces, just absolutely to pieces. The aviator was, of course, blown to pieces too. There wasn't anything to even pick up, I swear. So, that was one of the most terrible, terrible things to happen while I was out there.

And what I had not been aware of was that I was losing weight. Not from lack of food, there was plenty of food around. But I couldn't eat. It was sort of an emotional thing that was going on inside me. I had a typewriter that I traveled with, and I was sitting down writing these letters to everyone I knew back in the States. I wrote, "We're having very difficult times here—there's a great possibility that I will not be coming back, but I want you to know I've done my duty for God and country." [*Laughs*] Something like that. I would never mail those letters. I'd get it off my chest. But, as it was, I survived the whole thing.

I came back from the Philippines when the war was over, but I was still in uniform. I was here in San Francisco, and I thought I was going to be demobilized. But one of my female officers said, "Do you know that some of the women are still being sent to Europe?" And I said, "But the war is over." And she said, "Yes, but there's still positions over there for women and most of the WACs who are over there want to come home. So for awhile we're going to keep those openings for women over there." I said, "Gee, I'd love to do that." "You mean you don't want to get out?" I said, "No. I like this life." It was adventurous anyway. So, I signed up to continue in uniform, sort of a reenlistment, you might say, and I was sent over to London. I spent one year in London, and then I was sent to Paris for two years.

And it was in Paris that the United States Army—because you had a large occupying American colony there—said, "Anyone who wants to study French as long as they're in Paris can do so. It will be paid for by the government, and you will be delivered to L'ecole Alliance Francaise, *a la rive gauche*." We were 20 miles outside the city in an army encampment. So I signed up for that and was taken every day on the army buses into the city, and I'd go off to L'ecole Alliance Francaise, on the left bank, for my French class. It was two hours a day, five days a week. Well, there's no better place in the world to study French than France itself. You're in Paris, under French teachers, and you're living in a French world. I was fascinated by French; the very sound of it was like music.

It was in the classroom there, at L'ecole Alliance Francaise, that I met a German girl. [*Laughs*] One with hair under her arms. And she was from Munich. Her family apparently survived the war sufficiently well that they could finance her studies in Paris. She wanted to become an airline stewardess, and she felt it would be good to have a second or third language. She spoke excellent English. Well, I fell in love with her. We got to take our lunch together. She lived right there in the city, you know, and as time passed I began to say to myself, "I think I'm going to desert." It was growing on me. "The war is over, and I'm here in Paris. I'm still in uniform, but I've had enough of this damned army life, and I'm going to desert."

And I began to talk to Lisa—that was her name. I said, "I'm thinking of leaving the army." She'd say, "Oh, how interesting. Will you go back to the States?" I said, "No, you can get discharged right here!" Which is a damn lie. She didn't know anything about American military life. [*Laughs*] So I lied, sort of built it up that it was all right for me. And I moved in some civilian clothing, you know, and we decided to share expenses and live together. I had to drop out of school because the army came looking for me. I disappeared from my classes. That was going AWOL, Absent Without Official Leave, and you can be thrown into jail for that.

I ended up getting a dishonorable discharge over there in Paris. When I finally came forward and it was time to repatriate myself to the United States, I was called up for a court-martial. In World War II when we had 11 million people in the various military services, very few people actually were court-martialed. I happened to be one of them. They wanted to make an example of me.

How long did you live with Lisa?

M: Lisa and I lived together for a year and a half. I was AWOL for a year and a half. You know, at that time the Cold War with Russia was on, and anytime anybody disappeared from a military post the army thought that you had defected to the Russians. [*Laughs*] That was the last thing I was interested in, you know. The only reason I came forward was that I was running out of money. The money that I had earned back in San Francisco as a waitress was still in the bank, and so I had a little income coming in, and that's what I was living on. When that ran out I was a bit desperate.

When I finally went out to that army base outside of Paris after a year and a half, I still had my uniform, and they told me to put it on or I couldn't be there. So, I had to put my uniform on, and I was called in before a table of five female officers lined up there. They gave me this very formal parchment which said, "To Whom It May Concern, Miss Margaret Eloise Kennedy, on this date..." so and so, and all these formalities down to the end, "was given a dishonorable discharge." It was signed with all sorts of signatures, and it was stamped with governmental stamps.

I went outside after this thing was over, and I was reading this thing, and the commanding officer said to me, "You know, Kennedy, you're going to regret this! This is going to follow you through your life! This dishonorable discharge will pursue you. It's going to interfere with your chance of getting a job!" And to show you how brazen I could be—I was under a terrible strain, and I'm pretending now that I wasn't—I took this paper, right there in the midst of this officer, and I tore it to pieces! [*Laughs*] And I held my head high. She said, "How dare you! Look what you did with that; you're supposed to keep that thing!" So that was my disgrace there lying on the floor.

How old were you then?

M: Gad, I was about 33 or 34. They wouldn't let me stay in Paris. They sent me along with a couple of women officers down to the railroad station in Paris, and they put me on what they called the boat train. We journeyed from Paris to Le Havre, France, and there I got on that ship that brought me back. They just said, "You're not staying in Paris!" You see, I thought I'd get this discharge travel money, and then I could stay in Paris. But they wouldn't let me.

Was Lisa openly lesbian?

M: Well, we were having a lesbian relationship, but she had a lot of religious guilt. She was a very proper Catholic girl who would run off to Mass after we made love. We were from different cultures. I'll never forget her saying to me, "Margaret, when I see you stand in front of the mirror shaving off the hair under your arms, it makes me tremble with disgust!"

What happened to Lisa?

M: Well, that was the end of our relationship, but we continued by letter thereafter. Up to the time that I left the city, I continued to see her. But she knew I was going back to the United States, and she said, "I have a desire someday to go to the United States; maybe we can meet again there." That was the way we left it. What happened to her thereafter was she met an American soldier, had a sex relationship with him, and became pregnant. She gave birth to this illegitimate child, but by that time she was back home in Munich with her family. She had a son and gave it up for adoption, and she did become an airline stewardess.

You spent many years traveling, including 24 years at sea. During your times at home or ashore, did you ever want companionship, a relationship?

M: Yes. There were two periods when I lived with girls. Not only the one over in Paris, but here in the States. I lived with girls, shared an apartment with them, and both of them were disastrous. Absolutely disastrous.

How so?

M: Well, I don't know. In both instances we were just the wrong people for each other. One of them, she worked in a big insurance company in Boston, and I decided I'd settle in Boston for a while, and I went out and got a job in the city too, doing office work. And she said to me, "Let's go down and spend the summer in Cape Cod, at Provincetown." Well, Provincetown at that time was a gay town, and I understand it still is. It just swarmed in the summer season with homosexuals, male and female. So that's what we did; we went down there and rented a cabin for ourselves, and we began to quarrel. Oh. It wasn't a very happy day. So we broke up.

Another time was in Chicago; I lived with a girl there in an apartment. She used to taunt me. I liked her very much, but then she began to bring a boyfriend into the apartment, and she'd say to me, "Listen, can't you go out and get lost somewhere?" I'd say, "What? You mean you want me to go out so you can be alone with him?" I'd say, "No. I'm going to stay here." And we'd quarrel about that. And yet, she was a lesbian by all accounts. I guess she was bisexual.

I spent quite a few years just banging all over the world. I was in the Women's Army Corps. I've been to sea, and I went up to the Mississippi River and took a couple of turns at that, you know, and got a little, what you call a "beefsteak," stashed away. And about 16 years ago, I came back to San Francisco, and I checked into this building, and I've been here ever since. I have often looked at my life, saying I'm the world's outstanding failure at everything. And in other ways, I survived, so I wasn't really a failure when it came to that. I think too that I was always lucky; the only time I ever went without a job was when I didn't want one. [*Laughs*] But anytime I needed to get a job and hunker down and take care of myself, I always did.

Edythe Eyde
Burbank, California

When I arrive at Edythe Eyde's prewar bungalow in Burbank, Calif., Edythe, 69, is watching a daytime television talk show featuring a panel of women with outrageously-sized breasts.

I saunter down the path, past her 1965 Buick, Donnabell. A sticker in the rear window asks, "Have you hugged your pussycats today?"

It's a warm July afternoon. I am late, but Edythe's been amusing herself with Sally Jessy Raphael.

"Wanna Coke?" she asks, toddling off to the kitchen and returning with two glasses. She hands me one, and we focus our attention on the TV. "Wait a minute. I just want to see this part," she says.

"Oh, my God!" I gasp, ogling at one discussant with size 44EEE mammaries. "What in the world would anybody do with breasts that size?"

Edythe looks at me and winks: "Well, I don't know about you, but when I was younger, I would have had a hell of a good time!" She rolls her eyes in Eddie Cantor fashion and kicks one foot in the air.

This is quintessential Edythe: naughty and irrepressibly saucy, an authentic "hubba-hubba" gal. But there is something wounded about her too, which she does not readily show.

Born to an alcoholic father and compliant mother in rural Northern California, Edythe had no life of her own until she left her parents at nearly 30 years of age. The familial attitude toward her was summed up by an aunt who said, "It's plain you'll never amount to anything!"

Inside her worn one-bedroom, one-bath wood-frame house are modest belongings: a piano, television, books, records, a phonograph, and ceramic cat bric-a-brac. Her flesh and blood felines—17 in all, down from a one-time high of 35—are allowed everywhere but the living room, which is cordoned off by an elaborate screened door.

"I'm not replacing them as they die off because I'm old now too," says Edythe, giving me a tour of her home and leading me through to the back and side yards, which have been turned into an escape-proof cat pen complete with climbable table and chairs, a playhouse for shelter, and shelving that the cats gambol about on. "Who will take care of the younger ones when I pass? That concerns me."

Like many people her age, she lives alone, survives on Social Security, and takes most meals at a local cafeteria—$5.50, all you can eat. After more than 30 years as a secretary at Universal Studios and RKO, she retired at 65 and never looked back. A lifelong animal lover, she tends classroom pets at a local grammar school over school breaks and during the weekends.

"I feel sorry for those people who retire and feel lost," says Edythe. "I love being at home, reading, playing with my cats, talking to friends. I hated secretarial work. If I could have retired a day sooner, I would have."

Interviewed May 1990 and July 1995

It's a Jungle Out There:
Hollywood, the If Café, and I

You know, I guess I'll begin where I usually begin, which is, Where were you born?

E: Well, I was born in the Children's Hospital in San Francisco. And I spent my first three years in San Francisco, and then my family bought a fruit ranch, 33 acres, down on the Peninsula, and we all moved down there. So I was brought up in quite a rural section at the time. I can still remember one man still used a horse and buggy, and there were hitching rails, hitching posts, all along the main street of the town.

What year was that?

E: Oh, well let's see, must have been 1924. People were driving cars by then, the old-time Fords and Buicks, the real oldies that you see now in the car shows. And we had indoor plumbing, but the lady who was our nearest neighbor, who was several acres away from us, she had indoor plumbing, but she also had outdoor privies. And it was quite common around there for landowners—they might have indoor plumbing, but most of them had outdoor privies too. And many of them had their own cattle, their own cows for milk, and we had a goat for milk. And I grew up on real dairy cream and butter, the real stuff. If people used margarine back then, they were considered hard up.

I went to the grammar school there for seven years. I skipped one grade, so I was always a year younger than the rest of my class. I was fortunately born with the knowledge of how to read; no one ever had to teach me. I don't know, I just picked it up myself. But after I got in the third grade and they started math, I was at a loss, and I was one of the poorest students in math I remember, and I was poor in sports. I hated sports.

Did you like to write and play music even then?

E: Well, I loved music, but my parents were not musical; my dad couldn't carry a tune in a bucket. And my mother, you know, she'd sing while she was washing dishes or something, but there was no real knowledge or love of music in my family at all. They had an old Victrola, but their choice of music was just very, very, average. I didn't get interested in music until I got into grammar school, and then somebody handed me a violin, and I seesawed on that. I was certainly no prodigy, but I was always fooling around with it, and the teacher would say, "Now don't do that, just play what's there." You know, they discouraged me in every possible way from being creative.

And then I got into high school in a neighboring town. My first year was all right, but my second year, ah ha! That was great because I got into the high school orchestra, and I met my first love. Of course, I didn't know anything about anything. But it was she who initiated me in smooching. We didn't do anything below the belt, shall we say, but we smooched a lot and hugged and that sort or thing. And I thought that was just so much fun; I just loved it. She played violin too.

Every once in a while, Mother would ask me if I would like to have one of my little girlfriends come over to play, and I said,

"Yes." This went on from grammar school. There was no romance connected with it or anything because, of course, I was too young. But when I got into high school, I tried to have crushes on boys and things like that because I saw everybody else doing it. And I thought, *Well, he's a nice little boy; I'll smile at him and wave.* And he waves back or something, but I thought, *Oh, that's a bunch of crap, isn't it?* You know, I really didn't get into it.

But then when I hit it off with this gal; oh, I was so stupid. I told Mother, "Oh, I just love her; I just think the world of her." Course, I somehow knew that I shouldn't tell mother that we hugged. We would kiss a lot, but somehow I just kept that separate. And she'd bring her violin over, and we'd play the Bach double concerto and have a lot of fun with our music. Our music was a big part of it, you know. And then in my third year, we used to go behind the curtains of the small theater there and neck like crazy on our lunch hour.

And all of a sudden she stopped doing this and started going around with another little girl. She was a year older than I and *much* more developed than I. I was just a little, skinny runt, believe it or not. [*Laughs*] And I couldn't get over the fact that she had left me for this other girl. She wouldn't have lunch with me anymore. It just devastated me. And I told Mother, and Mother said, "What's the matter with you?" And I said, "Well, so-and-so doesn't want to have lunch with me anymore, and she is seeing a lot of this other girl, and it makes me feel terrible because she's my very best friend, and I just want to die."

And I just went on and on and on, you know. I was about 15, 14 and a half then, and Mother took it all in stride. I even wrote a song to the girl, and one day when Mother was fixing my hair—she used to always curl my hair and comb it for me—she said, "Say, you and so-and-so never did anything *wrong* together, did you?" I looked up at her and said, "*Wrong?* What do you mean?" It didn't occur to me there was anything *wrong* with it, you know. I thought she meant stealing something. And I looked at her,

"What do you mean?" And she never elaborated. Then after I got off by myself, I started thinking, and I thought, *Mother wants me for herself, or she's jealous or something.*

One thing Mother always wanted to do was read my mail. Now, I never wrote anything—any dirty stories or anything like that—in my letters to *anybody.* I never had any stories written to me in the mail. I guess that was what Mother was on the prowl for, I don't know. But I wasn't interested in smut, and that was the only thing she could think. She was not very knowledgeable about gay life or anything like that, and neither was I. But after I got to thinking about it, I thought, *Well, I better lay off of this because there is something different about it. All these other girls are interested in boys, and I'm not.* I was interested in music, so I addressed myself strictly to music.

Then I graduated from high school, and Mother kept me home two years. She didn't mention college to me, and I never thought of college. And my friend was long gone. I mean, I waited for her. I thought, *Well, I'll wait for her, and someday she'll come back.* I don't know why I believed this, but I did. I lived a very solitary life, and I didn't have any other girls my own age to speak with, compare my life to, and this is why I was so stupid as to wait and stay home with Mother.

So for two years, for my girlfriends and boyfriends, I had Mother. My dad was always off with business. When he'd come home, he never had kind words to say to me. I remember one time I said, "Hey, Dad, guess what? I got an A- in history!" or something I was bad at, and he says, "Next time get an A." That was his whole attitude throughout life to me, and if I were slumped over he would come up behind me and slap me square in the shoulders and say, "Straighten up! My sister died of TB, and you're going to too if you don't straighten up!" And one day he showed me a picture of some girl in a harness—a posture harness, and he said, "If you don't straighten up, that's what I'm going to get for you!" He never had a good word to say. But he never hit me or anything like that. He never raised a hand to me, but he could slap me down with a word.

Well then, after the two years, my mother said, "Would you like to go to college?" Now *they* always made the decision; I never was encouraged to think for myself—*ever*. "You do as you're told." "We will do this for you." And I was very—what's the word I want?—passive. I was very passive. As long as I was passive and didn't make waves, I got along fine with them.

But sometimes my mother would slap me across the face. She did this frequently—even after I got to be 16 or 17 years old. Not for swearing or anything like that—I wouldn't *dare*—but if I didn't want to help her with the dishes or I'd make some remark that was slightly sarcastic, *pow* across the face! They humiliated me a great deal when I was a child. Especially my father—he delighted in humiliating me in front of my little friends. And so I grew up as sort of a weirdo—not weirdo, but, you know, I wasn't with it. And then my mother said, "Would you like to go to college?" And I said, [*meekly*] "Well, all right." I can't believe I was that way now. So she sent me to a girls' college.

Where did you go?

E: Mills College. And the reason she did that was that my violin teacher taught at Mills.

What year was this that?

E: Oh, this was 1940 to 1942—I only went the two years. And I'm so sorry they did this because I did not have the brains to go to college. I didn't *care* whether I went to college or not, but it was nice to get away from them. I wasn't a brilliant student. I was good in music and English, but the rest of it was very average. And after two years I was not asked if I wanted to go back.

By your parents?

E: Yeah, by my parents. I went there on a scholarship anyway, and I worked in the library to help pay for my tuition. So I just sort of moseyed along with the time and wondered what was going to happen next, but I didn't care much. And the reason I didn't care much was I had lost my friend in high school, and after that I really didn't give a hang much about what happened. And this went on for about seven years.

Did you ever think of women during that time? Think of pretty girls, other girls?

E: No. I was attracted to their looks in college, but I didn't do anything about it because they all had their minds on boys, and none of them would honey up to me. Now, if I had had one that, you know, cruised me, or came into my room and hugged me or something, then that would have been a *different* story. But I was not one to initiate *anything*, you know. I just lay back and let things happen because that's the way I was brought up to do. So nothing happened in college.

Then I was back home with Mother and Daddy, and I thought, *I'll just keep taking lessons from the man up there at his home, and I won't go to college anymore.* But the next thing I knew, my dad took me over to the business college in the neighboring town. And he said, "We're going to enroll you in this now." So I thought, *Well, all right.* So I went over there to business college, and I learned how to type and how to take shorthand. I wasn't very interested, but I applied myself because I was expected to; and I was one of the best in that class.

It was never considered that you might be a professional musician or something?

E: Apparently not, although I practiced diligently.

Did you consider leaving home?

E: No-o-o. Oh, I wouldn't have dared. I wouldn't know how to take care of myself. I mean, Mother always fixed my hair. I didn't even know how to go to a store and shop for groceries or anything. Mother did all of that.

How old were you?

E: I was 21, believe it or not. But Mother always kept me a child. I can remember at 18 or so, Mother said, "Remember, you're just a child, you're just a child." They kept me so subdued that it didn't occur to me that I didn't know how to go out and do these things. I never had any thought of doing anything with my life except living with them. That's how subdued I was, how subjugated I was.

Your parents, given that they wanted you to be reliant upon them, probably liked the fact that you weren't interested in boys.

E: Yeah, probably. Oddly enough, marriage was never pushed at me, and I think one reason was that Mother really wasn't very happy. My parents never fought. There was never any domestic violence or quarreling or anything like that at home. If they had any discussions, it was after Mother sent me to bed. I always had to go to bed by 9:30 P.M., even after I came home from college. [*Laughs*]

How did you get the idea to escape from your parents to Southern California?

E: In college I started writing letters to people who had their names and addresses in science fiction and fantasy magazines. Boys and girls—these were not old men. And I got to writing especially to one chap who lived down here, and I thought, *Gee, that would be just jolly if I could move down here and get away from my parents.* So I did.

That was quite a big step from the Peninsula down to Southern California.

E: Well, yeah, it was. And I would never have made it if Mother and I hadn't driven down here when I was in my teens for a vacation one time. Dad had to stay at home on the ranch to take care of things, but Mother and I took off and came down here. I was at the age where Hollywood was all glamour to me and "Oh, gee whiz! Look at that," you know. I was real naive, and I guess my mother was too. We took a little room down here. She left off slapping me around, and we had some fun. We had some good times too. She spoiled it all by all that slapping and instilling me with guilt feelings and things like that. It was not a happy life.

Anyway, after I'd settled here, I went up north to visit them—I think I was 27 or 28 at the time. I went up on the bus. And that was the year Mother said to me, "Edythe, have you been to the doctor?" And I said, "Doctor? I'm not sick." But they arranged for me to have a complete physical examination because I hadn't been to a doctor for 12 years. So I thought, "OK. Great. I won't have to pay for it. It might be a good idea." So Mother said, "Well, you really don't have to go through with this, you know, unless you have something to *hide.*" And then it dawned on me why she wanted me examined by a doctor.

She wanted to make sure you were still a virgin.

E: Yes. I never lost my virginity, at that time, when I was down here. It didn't occur to me that I would want to do so. Why should I want to bring another child into the world? I was miserable enough. Well, its true! That's the way I always thought. So I went, and my dad brought me to the doctor. And I had to subject myself to all sorts of things. Well, I mean, I had a complete physical, including something else, which I had never heard of before, and I was humiliated to tears. And the doctor took an awful lot of blood out of my leg. I said, "My goodness! What do you want so much blood for? He said, "Well, we're giving you a Wassermann test." That's the kind of a test to see if you have bad diseases, I guess. I was so shocked, it just blurted out. I said, "My God, what kind of a girl do they think I am?"

When I was 29 my mother went to the hospital, and she died of colon cancer. I don't think she had the will to live anymore anyway. I was gone from her life. She used to live through me, exclusively, I'm sure. She had no other interests.

Where were you working at that time?

E: Oh, I was working at an office here in Burbank as a secretary.

The very thing that you hated.

E: Yeah, well I worked 39 years at the very thing I hated, but I was a darn good secretary.

You were cloistered, a passive young woman who lived with her parents, and who, even when she wasn't living with her parents, was pretty much dominated by her parents. But also you published the first lesbian magazine, Vice Versa. *So I want to know what happened? How did you go from very subjugated young woman to lesbian publisher, bon vivant and gay community darling?*

E: Well, I didn't know I was all that! [*Laughs*] I lived in a series of small rooms when I came down here. In one of them there were some women who lived upstairs, and we all used to sun-bathe on the roof of the garage of the place. I love to lie in the sun. So I took my little blanket out there one day and lay down. These three girls that lived upstairs said, "Hi," and I said, "Hi." I had brought a book, and I was reading, and I noticed that they all just talked about girls. And I thought, "Gee, that's nice; you don't have to hear all this talk about dates and pregnancies and this, that, and the other."

So I got to chatting with them. One thing led to another, and I mentioned something about not caring about dates or some-thing; I can't remember how it started. These girls looked at me and said, "Are you gay?" I said, "Well, I try to be as happy as I can under the circumstances." And they all sort of snickered, and I didn't quite know what they meant—and yet I did. But I wasn't going to commit myself. So then they explained, and I said, "Oh yes, I feel very much that way too, but I don't know anyone." They said, "Well, come with us next Saturday, and we'll take you to a place. And how would you like to go to a softball game with us?" I said "OK." Actually, I hate sports, but I was interested in going and meeting a lot of...[*Makes a clicking sound*] So I went to the softball game and was bored out of my skull by all of those girls running around, but some of them did have nice legs. [*Laughs*] I enjoyed watching them bat the ball. So I got introduced to a few of them, and nothing came of that. But they took me down to a place called the If Café on Vermont Street down here in L.A.

What year was that?

E: That was about 1946 or 1947. And when we walked in, there were several girls dancing together, and I thought, *Gee, how nice!* And as we eased ourselves into a booth, why, somebody came out carrying a birthday cake with candles, and they sang "Happy Birthday" to some girl with it, and my ol' eyes just brimmed with tears, and I thought, *Oh, isn't this wonderful to be among girls who* *like girls!* You know, I'd never seen anything like it. So I got up and had a few dances with them. Some of the cute things would come over to me and say, "Would you care to dance?" [*Grins*] And I'd say, "Mm-hmm," and I'd go and dance. So I came back there again and again and again. I thought it was a wonderful place.

Actually, looking back, it was a dive. The girls were allowed one half of it, and they danced, but there were some fellas and people off the street that would come in and sit on the bar side and look at us gals as we were dancing. But men were not permitted by the owner to come around and ask us to dance. That's one thing. The owner's name was Barney, and he'd say, "No, no. This is the men's side; that's the women's side." But the men's side was not for gay men. The men's side was for ordinary guys.

A little bit before that time, I got the idea that there should be a gay magazine for girls. I started this magazine before I knew any girls. But I had to have sort of a fantasy life because I wasn't having much of a life that way of my own, so I devised this little magazine. At the time I was working at a place where the boss was out a lot. And he said, "I don't care what you do, as long as you look busy. If you get your work done, then you can type personal letters or anything like that, but I don't want you sitting around reading books and magazines. As long as you look busy, I don't care." So I devised this little magazine. I would type reams and reams of stories and things, and he never asked what I was typing or anything; he didn't care as long as I got my work done. Well, I'd get my work done first, and I got to be a real split-second typist doing this, you know. So, I got the carbon paper they had in those days—they didn't have duplicating machines—and I would run it through eight copies at a time, twice. This was a heck of a lot of work. Then I would go and filch some Manila folders from the supply, and I would put all these pages in there, nice and neat, staple them together. Voilà! I had a magazine! I thought, *Well, I'll save these magazines, and then when I meet some girls, I'll distribute them.*

So when I met these girls, I distributed these magazines. Of course, they were very homemade, you know. They were very primitive, but you didn't have computers, and electric typewriters were unknown in those days—you used a manual. So that's why this was so primitive, and I had no guidelines to go by; I just had to sort of make them up in my head as I went along.

Well, I would ask these girls, as I got to know them later, "Come on now, submit a story." Or, "Wouldn't you like to write a poem or movie review or something for this magazine?" "Oh, yeah, I'll think about it." They were too busy living it to care. But they always wanted the magazine. I gave it away; I never charged for it because it was a labor of my heart, and I felt that it would be almost like being a prostitute to charge. In the magazine too, somewhere in the pages, I said, "Now, when you get through with this, don't throw it away; pass it along to the next girl, keep it going, because I may not always be able to write these." And that was very prophetic because after that job terminated there, I wasn't.

How many issues did you do?

E: I think I did eight or nine of them. I would get an occasional submission of something or other, which I was really honor-bound to print, no matter how bad it was, and I used no names— there was no "poem by so-and-so, story by so-and-so"; you couldn't tell who wrote what because I thought I better not use names. In those days everything had to be rather hush-hush. I didn't even mention Los Angeles or San Francisco; you couldn't tell what city the magazine came from. But I would go down to the If Café and pass these things out until one of the girls told me, "Hey, you shouldn't bring those things here because if they catch you with them, they'll put you in jail." And I said, "What?" "Yeah, they'll put you in jail!" I said, "Why? There's no four-letter words or dirty stories in it." She said, "It doesn't matter—if it's gay, they'll put you in jail." So that tipped me off, and I didn't do that anymore. I used to blithely mail them out through the mail. Gee, I was naive. They had no pictures in them; the stories were not sexy at all, you know. But these girls put me wise. So then I just handed them out personally to people when I would meet them somewhere else; I didn't mail them out anymore.

I went back to the If for quite a while and met quite a few gals there, and then they would ask me out on dates, and that was fun. They had different gay places. There were some down Santa Monica Beach, and I would go down there; they were all dives, though. I remember one time especially at the If. There were a group of us at the booth, and the other four got up to dance, two by two, and I was left by myself for that one number, and I was sipping a Coke. I didn't drink because I thought, *Well, if they do raid the place and they catch me, at least I'll have my brain on straight.* So I would always drink a soft drink. So, along comes this guy—he wanders over from the bar, and Barney doesn't see him. He stops at the first booth and talks to the girls, then he bumbles on to the second booth and talks to some of them, and I see them shake their heads. So l thought, *Uh-oh, he wants to dance.* So he came over to me. He was inebriated. And he said, "Care to dance, lady?" I said, "No, thank you." And I sipped my Coke. "Oh, come on. Just a little dance." I said, "I don't care to dance, thank you." He leans over to me, and he put his old dirty hand on the table, and he leered at me and says, "What's the matter, lady? Don't you dance with *men?*" At that point I got angry, and I said, "Of course not! What kind of a girl do you think I am!" He just took off. And as I said that, the other two couples came back, and they looked at me. "What did you say to him?" I said, "Well, he wanted to dance and wanted to know if I danced with men, and I said, 'No, what kind of a girl do you think I am?'" And they said, "You didn't say that?" I said, "I certainly did! It got rid of him, didn't it?" That's a true story.

It seems it's hard enough to find nice girls to go out with today. How in the world did anyone find women to go out with in the 1940s and

1950s, when everything was much more secretive and quiet?

E: Well, the way that most of us found them, and the way that I found them, was that I went down to the gay bars. And in those days, of course, we didn't have the drug scene and all that tawdry business. When you went to a gay bar in those days, you went to drink beer and to smoke, and that was about the worst thing the girls ever did. And you found a lot of really nice gals down there and some that were not so nice and some who were just there to look at how the other half lived. But among them there was always someone you could jibe with and talk with. And if they liked you enough and you liked them enough, you asked them over to your room or your apartment or whatever you happened to be living in at the time. And they would have parties at different places and invite more girls, and we'd take it from there. And we met some very nice people that way.

Of course, that was the only way you *could* meet back then. But the secretiveness was not continued in the bars. You know, I mean, if you went there, it was no secret! [*Laughs*] So I found it very easy to meet people that I would enjoy dating—and being dated by, I should say—because I was feminine, and I still am. And it was no problem.

Today, I imagine, it would be harder because there's such a variety of women who call themselves lesbians, and here you find out that they have a husband and a couple of kids in the background. Or maybe they're recovering from the dope scene or something, and, I mean, who needs it? I don't. If I were a young squirt today, I wouldn't want to get mixed up with somebody who had a husband and couple of kids, and I certainly would steer shy of anyone who was dependent on drugs of any sort because it renders them so stupid and so vulnerable to the world at large! I mean, it's a jungle out there. There are lots of people looking for someone who's under the influence of drink or something that they can take advantage of. Who wants to be that way? Who wants to be with anyone who's that way? I don't!

In the bars of the era, surely there must have been some women who led double lives, who had husbands but would go to lesbian clubs. Or were those women known by the other women and generally steered clear of?

E: Well, I really don't know because I never met anyone who confessed to me that they were that way. Now, maybe they were that way, and they didn't confess to me, but I never got intimate with anybody like that. There was, at one place, this girl and her husband, who was gay, but he was her husband. They were terrific dancers. They would go to the bars, and they'd dance—he with the he's, and she with the she's. I loved to dance with her, but I wouldn't think of striking up a cozy acquaintance with her.

Because she had a husband?

E: Because she had a husband! That spoiled it for me. I wasn't that way—I didn't have any boyfriends on the side—and I didn't want anybody that way. To me they were—well, it's a funny word—*contaminated,* so to speak. [*Laughs*] To me, gay was *gay,* by golly, and I didn't mix the two! Now, I know today they say most people are bisexual. That's the trend, the fancy thing to be, but I was never that way, and I was never attracted to anyone I knew who was that way, and I still like to keep it that way. I guess I'm a separatist in that way; however, I love my gay brothers.

The gay boys would always say, "Well, my company is having its annual banquet at such-and-such, and we have to show up with a girlfriend; would you go with me that night?" And I'd say, "Sure," and I'd go and have a ball! I would get into a dress—well, I mean, I always wore dresses anyway—and shamble on down there with him and sit at the table, and everybody that he associated with at the office just assumed that I was his girlfriend. We didn't camp it up or smooch or do anything like that; we didn't put on an act. At least he was able to be seen there with a girl that looked like a girl. Then he would take me home, say good-bye at the door, and away he would go to the gay bars for the boys, and I would go home by myself, you know. But I was very happy with this arrangement, and so were they. It worked out just great.

In those days, if you were a man, you didn't dare let on. You had to really keep up an act. It wasn't like today at all. I never dreamed that I'd see the day when people would be outspoken about it at the office. I mean, in my day, if you were they would fire you. "No queers around here; we don't need your kind!" You had to stand for it; I mean, you just did.

And did you ever take a fellow to an office function?

E: I think that I had a buddy that I took to a function one time too. He looked very ordinary, but you had to do that in those days—to just show up with somebody. We didn't make a terrific show of affection or anything silly like that; we just enjoyed our-selves and had a good time. [*Laughs*]

You said that when you would go to functions, you looked femme. What does that mean for you?

E: Looking femme?

Yes.

E: Are you speaking of office functions or gay functions?

Anywhere.

E: Oh. At office functions I'd always wear a dress and earrings and stuff. I've always, more or less, dressed that way. I dress to please myself. I don't dress to please the crowd. That's the way I always was. And then for some of the picnics and gay things, I'd always wear slacks—or in the days when my legs were not covered with purple veins, why, I'd wear shorts, a little halter or something. I always looked feminine, but that's the way I wanted to be. And I never cared about trimming my hair short or anything like that because that just wasn't me.

I remember one time at the If Café, or one of those places, I was dancing with a big, tall masculine-looking girl. And she was heads above me, and she looked down at me and beamed, and I smiled up at her. And she said, "What are you here for honey? Just to see how the other half lives?" And I looked up at her and said, "Why, no!" I said, "I'm just as gay as you are!" You know, it astounded me that she would think that I was just in masquerade or something! [*Laughs*] And she laughed, and I laughed because I wasn't indignant; I was just surprised. It didn't occur to me that I should dress any differently, and of course nobody wanted me to because all the gay girls down there wanted a girl who looked like a girl. They didn't really want somebody striding in there in boots and jeans and a short hair cut when they were looking for a girlfriend. That's the way it was in those days. Now of course it's a bit different. They don't have that butch/femme thing anymore. But I was always femme, and I've always felt that way—even up to my older years now. I'm just me. And if they don't like it, they can lump it. [*Laughs*]

Given that you were femme, did women ask you out, or did you ask them out, typically?

E: They asked me out. Once in a while—after I got to know them, of course—I would ask them because they'd asked me, and I'd say, "Well, gee, I have some tickets for thus and so. Would you like to go with me?" And then, of course, I'd ask them out, but I never marched up to a stranger and said that. I had to know them first.

I had to be going with them first. But they'd done so many nice things for me, you know, that I'd like to pay them back once in a while.

And would you go to a regular restaurant, let's say, if you were going to have a date?

E: Oh, yeah. I can remember one time—this lady was reputed to be a terrifically wealthy gal. She was years older than I. She was at this private party, and the hostess who lived there said—I can't remember this woman's name—she says, "This lady would like to ask you out for dinner this evening." And I said, "Well, why doesn't she come up and ask me?" [*Laughs*] And she did, and I said, "Yes, I'd love to go out." She took me to Perino's on Wilshire. And I was told by the hostess that she was really loaded. So I said yes, if she wanted to go there. I'd never been there, but of course I'd heard of it. And we marched in there and had a very lovely dinner at Perino's. Of course, it was the only time I ever went!

And what did she look like, your partner for the evening?

E: Oh, she was rather heavyset. Not fat, but an older, middle-aged person. Very neat. Very well-dressed. Nothing to really faint over, you know. But she was very presentable and very nice, and I liked her company very much. I wasn't attracted to her, but after all, if she was going to invite me out to dinner, I wasn't going to say no.

In some ways she was taking a big chance, wasn't she? How did she know you were a lesbian?

E: Because I was at this private party, and nobody got in there unless they were gay or lesbian. Nobody. This was not a bar; this was a private party. I went to many, many private parties there hosted by these two gals. And anyone there was safe.

So there was no risk.

E: No. No risk at all.

Did it ever happen that you were asked out by a woman not in a gay or lesbian setting? Someone who took a big risk in approaching you?

E: No. I can't remember that I ever was. Because I usually saw to it that I was in gay and lesbian settings. That's what I wanted. And why would I go to heterosexual parties? They bored me. And I knew that if I did, I would be hit upon—approached, I should say—by some straight guy, and I didn't want anything to do with them. I mean, I was friendly and cordial and polite to them, but I sure as hell didn't want to go out on a date with them! [*Laughs*]

Well, if you went out with a more butch woman—let's say to Perino's or some other restaurant—did heads turn, would people look?

E: No, I don't think so. I wasn't really watching for that. I strolled in there and sat down, and I didn't think once about, "Gee, I wonder if someone is watching me?" It just didn't occur to me. I mean, after all, if she had the money to pay for the dinner and we were dressed decently, why should anyone bother? I could have been her daughter or her niece or somebody, I suppose. I mean, she wasn't dressed in boots and chaps or something! [*Laughs*]

In those days you couldn't go to a gay and lesbian bookstore and buy literature such as Valerie Taylor's or Isabelle Miller's novels.

E: No, you couldn't.

Literature that represented gay and lesbian people as just people. Most of the stuff about us in movies and in books presented us as being pathological.

E: Yeah.

Crazed in some way.

E: Oh, yeah. [*Groans*]

What did you and your peers think of those images? Did you laugh at them? Did you take them to heart?

E: Well, I got awfully sick of these stories where one of the girls would end off marrying somebody, or the other one would go off and kill herself. And if I knew that was the kind of story it was, I wouldn't even bother with it. And then a bunch of cheap literature turned up at the drugstore, and anybody could go into the drugstore and buy one of those. So I'd read those, but I thought that most of them were pretty trashy and tawdry at the time. I read a few of them, but I didn't make a collection of them because I didn't want them around the apartment or wherever I was living at the time. I certainly didn't take any of them to heart!

The only thing I thought was, *Maybe we never grew past the teenager stage.* Perhaps we were—what's the word I want?—not retarded in our emotional growth but along in there. Because that was the prevailing opinion of the time in different articles that appeared in the more serious things like *Reader's Digest* or some psychology magazines. The doctors believed that we hadn't quite matured enough to go on with a heterosexual relationship. And I thought at the time, *Well, that may very well be true. I don't know whether it is or not, but it certainly is better than being thought crazy or perverted or sinners or something.* And I thought, *Well, if that's the way they believe, that's well and good. I know how I feel, and that's the way I'm going to be.*

So you really weren't negatively affected by these images. As far as you know, you just took them with a grain of salt.

E: That's right.

When all of the images one sees of oneself are negative, it takes a lot of character not to fall into thinking, Oh, I must be that.

E: Well, I don't know. I was by myself by that time. I'd run away from my parents. Perhaps if I'd had parents who were nagging at me and holding up these people as negative examples or something, maybe I would have had a few more doubts. But I didn't. I was away from them, and all I knew was that I was having a heck of a lot of fun at the time! I was young then and got around a lot, and why should I be unhappy about it? You know, it brought me nothing but fun and games and laughter, and I was never in serious raids or anything like that, so why not go along with it? That's the way I felt. I wasn't going to change because some book said I was a certain way. What do they know? They aren't me. So I was never particularly militant about it; I was just sort of self-accepting.

When I walk down the street in L.A. today, it's not unusual for me to see women whom I can identify. I see women holding hands; it's all very out. And I'm sure that there was a kind of a subculture. You knew where to go to find those girls.

E: Well, you heard from one girl to the other; you didn't know instinctively where to go, but if someone at a certain gay bar might say, "Well, have you been to this gay bar yet? It's over on Wilmington, and the name of it is such-and-such." Then you'd go there, and they'd say, "Oh, well, but have you been to the one on Normandie." That's the way you learned—from word of mouth.

And you were never involved in any raids? I know they were quite common in those days.

E: No, I never was, except for one time down on the beach. I had gone there just to see what was what, and I didn't usually go into this place. They had dancing, but there was something about the place that didn't attract me a lot.

Was it in Santa Monica?

E: Yeah. So I went in there, and I saw a couple of girls I knew sitting at a table. So I went over to their table, sat down, and ordered a 7UP. And I hadn't been there long, but a bunch of policeman came in, and I thought, *Uh-oh.* I had on slacks, but I had on my little red, sparkly earrings and some beads, I think, or a froufrou blouse to go with them and long hair, you know. And the police came over with tablets and pencils, and they said, [*gruffly*] "What's your name?" And the music was playing so loud. So when they got to me I looked them right in the eye and said, "My name is Edythe Eyde!" And he said, "What's that? And I said, "*Edythe Eyde!*" Well, they couldn't tell. And he wrote something down, but I knew damn well that he didn't write anything [real] down. He couldn't tell my name or how it was spelled, and I wasn't going to spell it for him.

So then he went on to somebody else because he'd got a look at my long hair and earrings and decided I wasn't one of *those.* So then he went to a bunch of boys, and they were all sitting around a table. And there was one guy—of course, boys in those days didn't wear long hair—and this guy had kind of a...I guess he hadn't had a haircut in a while, but it looked like a man's haircut, but you couldn't tell really whether he was a dyke or a guy. And he had a bright red shirt on. But he was a guy. So the police gathered around him in a circle. I had the uncomfortable feeling that they made him take his pants down to see if he was a boy or a girl. I didn't look too closely because I would have been too embarrassed, but they hid him from us anyway. And then they let him sit down again. But I thought, *What a humiliating thing if that is what really happened.* So then the cops stomped out. And I said, "Well, girls, I think I'll go home." And they said, "Oh, don't go yet." And I said, "Why?" And they said, "Because they lurk outside, and if anyone leaves early, then they harass them again." So I waited a full half hour or so before I left, and then I got in my car and drove home. I never went back to that place again.

Do you remember the name of it?

E: I can't remember it. It was right on the beach in one of those great, big old buildings. And I think they had dancing there. They sure had a loud jukebox. That was in the 1950s.

That experience frightened you?

E: Yeah. And it was the 1950s because in the 1960s I was living here, and I had quit going to the bars because there was no reason to do it. I was here, and I had a bunch of friends, and that was it.

Did you meet women at work? There's what we call gaydar—I sort of see you, and I know it.

E: Yeah!

Did you have that sense with women?

E: Oh, yeah! I sure did! I mean, I could walk down the street, and I'd go *ph-h-h-ht!* [*eyes riveting on an imagined woman*]. It was uncanny, you know. And then when I quit being social altogether, I lost it. But I still have it a little bit today, but not much because I don't use it much. But in the old days, it was right out there like antennae on a butterfly! [*Laughs*]

And at work did you meet women?

E: No. I was very careful at work not to appear gay. You had to be if you wanted to keep your job, especially at Universal. Because by then everybody knew [the word] gay, and at my age if I weren't married, they might think of it—even though you didn't dress that way. Of course, at work I always wore the jewelry and the secretarial outfit and all that stuff. I always did anyway.

So, if someone found out you were gay, you could be fired?

E: I suppose. Yeah. They might have suspected it. I know there was one girl there—oh, she had sex on her mind all the time. She'd tell dirty jokes. And she was such an attractive girl too. She was always fixing up her girlfriends with dates at work, and then the girlfriends would come back and tell her what happened, and then she'd tell everyone else what happened—you know, whether they slept with them that night and all that. I thought she was a dreadful person. Well, apparently, she might have gotten it in her head that I was gay, I don't know, but one time in her office she put her arm around me and cuddled me close, and I knew she wasn't gay, and I didn't want anything to do with her. And I pretended that she had tickled me on the ribs, and I went, "Ah ha ha ha!" And I gave her a real good jab in the ribs with my elbow. And she said, "Ow! Oh, God, that hurt!" "And I said, "Oh, I'm so sorry, Beverly. I'm terribly sorry, but I'm so ticklish, and you know how that is." And she never did that again.

What do you think she was after?

E: Oh, she wanted to find out whether I'd snuggle back or something, I guess. I don't know. But I didn't want any part of her. She was a creep. And she was pretty. She could attract the boys like bees to honey. But I didn't want anything to do with her. And she gossiped too, about people. "Oh, you know so-and-so—he's gay." You know, some publicist or something. And she said that in front of some other secretaries, and I said, "You don't know that for sure. You could get him in trouble and lose him his job saying a thing like that! How do you know for sure? Did you see him?" And she'd shut up.

Well, now we hear that there were stars of that era who were lesbians— Agnes Moorehead, Barbara Stanwyck, for instance.

E: Oh, you hear stories, but you know, after they're dead what can they do to refute the stories? I hate that. I really do. I've never heard it about Agnes Moorehead. I've heard it about Barbara Stanwyck. But I don't now whether she ever got married or not. Maybe she didn't, and that's why they said it. Maybe she wouldn't shell out, and maybe they said she was gay because she wouldn't go to bed with so-and-so. You know? What difference does it make? They're gone. They said that about Lizabeth Scott too. But I think that was true in her case because when I was at RKO, I saw her flouncing around one of the streets with a girl-friend, arm and arm, real cozy. I looked at her, and my little antennae went out, and I knew. She was really interesting looking. She was not really beautiful, but she had a striking visage on her. I liked her looks very much. In fact, if she had come up to me and said, "You want to go to dinner tonight?" I'd have said, "Well sure! Let's go!" [*Laughs*]

How was it that you began to write and perform gay and lesbian parodies of popular songs?

E: I took up the guitar at the suggestion of a lady that I was very smitten with. She was years older than I, but I loved her mind. She was very intelligent. She was completely different from the callow young girls that I ran with. I was very impressed by her because she owned her own home, and she had a substantial position in a movie studio. She just completely unglued me. I wasn't smitten with her in a sexual sense; I was just smitten. It didn't have anything to do with sex. I don't know. I guess I was looking around, maybe even for a parental figure to worship because my own two parents were so much the opposite.

Anyway, she said, "When you write songs, you should really learn to play the guitar." And I was up there at one of her parties, and there was an elderly Spanish lady, nongay, who was up there, and she had a guitar and she was singing all these Spanish songs. And then she would forget her lyrics once in a while, and I would chime in with the Spanish lyrics because I had learned these songs in high school years ago, and I remembered them. And she'd say, "Oh, yes, that's the way it goes." I practically sat through the entire party while my friend and her cronies were drinking beer and smoking and playing cards, which didn't interest me in the least. I sat with this elderly lady, and we sang songs. I watched her play the guitar, and I thought, "I betcha I could do that too!" I can usually play anything that I have a mind to 'cause I have an ear for it.

So two weeks later, I guess it was, I went down to a swap shop, and I traded a portable dishwasher I'd won on a radio show for a guitar that they had hanging up there. It wasn't much of a guitar, but I didn't know the difference. The man threw in a book of hillbilly songs with it, and away I went. I went home and I looked through this book and I thought, *Well, that's not the kind of song I really want to sing,* like "Comin' 'Round the Mountain" and all that. I had nothing against it, but I wanted to sing my own songs. So I started from scratch and tried to find all these notes on the strings of the guitar; I didn't get anywhere for about the first two weeks. And then all of a sudden I found some chords. And then I learned one song and then two songs.

Then I went up to my friend's place and sang for her and had the gratification of seeing her eyes light up and a big smile on her dear face. I thought, *Oh, I'm so glad I learned this.* So then I wrote her a few songs. She, at the time, was smitten with an older woman who had been nongay and married for a while. She was a very experienced person. It broke my heart to see my friend go gaga over somebody who, in my humble opinion, was not worth her. You know, used merchandise. At least that's the way I thought of it at the time, which was probably prompted by pangs of jealousy. But I never said anything against her or anything like that, but it hurt me.

I went on with the guitar anyway, and I soon began getting invitations to play at this party or that party, and I knew a lot of gay men too. And they were an awfully nice bunch of fellas; the ones that I knew, they would give fabulous parties.

So anyway, I got asked around to different places to play and sing. One thing, at the Flamingo when night came and the nongay people would come in—the afternoons were for *us*—these gay professional entertainers would get up there on that little stage, and they would say the most deprecating things about themselves. Run themselves down. I remember one time, one gay man was dressed up as a woman and said something terrible about the lady singer, who was a very good singer. I wouldn't even repeat it, it was so bad. Well, I will repeat it, just to give you an idea of how crummy. He said, "Oh, she's so butch that when she has her monthly, she wears a band aid." I thought, "Oh, God!" And the straights were sitting around, "Ha ha ha ha," you know; and the more these people would talk down about themselves, the more laughter would come from these other people. I thought, *My God! Why do these gay people do that? I think that is terrible to make a buck at the expense of their own dignity. Where are their brains?*

Well anyway, I was so revolted by that—revolted is the word—that I decided that I would write a few gay parodies. But they weren't going to down-speak us. They were going to be upbeat songs. They were going to be gay songs; they were not going to be full of four-letter words, but they were going to be gay. So I wrote a few parodies, and I sang them at a gay spot. I didn't pretend to be a singer or a professional or anything, but this was just for the gays. And boy, did they clap—because they liked the idea of something positive. It wasn't that I was so great or the words were so great, but they liked the idea of something positive being sung up there.

So I wrote a few more gay parodies like that, and after that I got invited to party after party. "Bring your guitar, sing your songs," you know. I had a lot of fun doing it, but I never did it professionally.

You performed under a stage name?

E: No, I performed under my own name, but someone had told a nongay man who was making an album, about me. He phoned me and wanted to know if I would make a recording or be part of the album, just part, do one song. So I said yes. I was to meet him at Capitol Records there in Hollywood. I thought, *Wait a minute. What am I saying? I can't do this.* Because my parents were alive at the time, and I don't have a name like "Margaret Smith" or, you know, something that was common—"Oh, that's not *that* person; that's somebody with a name *like* hers." So, I thought, "Well, what will I do?" So I thought of the name Lisa Ben because it's an anagram. Well, you can see it in your mind—it spells *lesbian.* So I thought I'll take that name, just use Lisa Ben. I didn't want to go by that name or have my friends all of a sudden call me Lisa instead of my real name, but my name would be on that record, and the record was going to be distributed, supposedly, all over the country.

So I went to Capitol Records. It was during the time the Beatles were here, and the man said, as he led me in the studio, "The Beatles just left here!" The studio—the mikes and everything—were still warm from them. He said, "Aren't you impressed?" And I said, "No." [*Laughs*] I didn't like them. I never have, and I never will. So he sat me down, and I rattled off a song, and it went just fine. They had a technician in the studio who was pressing but-

tons and doing all sorts of this and that. And I'd never seen anything like that before, but I just sort of shut my eyes to it so I
wouldn't be distracted, and I did my "Frankie and Johnny." And
the guy in the booth says, "Perfect. Great!" And the other guy
says, "Do you want to do it over again?" And I said, "Why? It went
all right." I was so offhand about it. I can't believe that I was that
way now because here was all this technical paraphernalia, and a
guy to run it, and I was so unimpressed. Nobody told me to be
afraid. But they didn't include my song on the album; the album
was mainly for gay boys, and they wanted men on the album. So
I thought, *Oh, well. That's life.*

Do you remember the title of it? The album?

E: No, I don't. I have a copy of it somewhere, but I don't think I
could ever find it right now. Anyway, it was all full of parodies, but
it was all men. And a short while later, they put my record out as
a single and sold it overseas. And every once in a while I'll get—oh,
about twice a year—maybe $18, $15, $20, or something from
record sales overseas. I get just a very small percentage of it. But
this has continued through the years. So once in a while I get a little trickle of money in—not that it matters to a hill of beans, but it's
encouraging, you know. But that's how I got the name Lisa Ben.

In 1989 I was asked to be a part of a lot of performers who
played for a lesbian group down in Culver City. Southern California for Women or something, and some lady phoned me—I'd
never heard of her—and she was in charge of the whole program.
She asked me if I would do some of my parodies. So I said, "Oh,
yeah. I guess so; I haven't practiced for a little while." But I sat
down afterwards and practiced a few of them, and went down
there and did them. And I thought there'll probably be a jolly little group like I'm used to playing for. A "jolly group" turned out
to be 450 in a huge auditorium, and I was just petrified.

Fortunately, two gals brought me down because I don't drive

at night very much anymore because sometimes the lights bother me—especially if I get very excited, which I was that night—and I can't judge distances too well. They came clear over from Altadena, bless 'em, darling girls, and took me down there and took me back, which was quite a bit out of their way. But it was a marvelous program, and I felt a little bit out of my class because quite a few of the women there were professional entertainers. So by the time I got up there, I felt sort of foolish, you know, because here I am with a guitar and homemade songs.

Well, I went through with it, and I gained a little confidence as I went on. I sang some parodies that I just wrote the lyrics to, and then I sang the song that I wrote, "A Fairer Tomorrow." When I sang that—I wrote that from the heart, tune and lyrics—much to my surprise, they all stood up and gave me a standing ovation. I was so moved, you know. I said, "Sit down; I'm not worth that!" [*Laughs*] It really gave me a great feeling because I don't do this to boost my own ego, really. I just do it because I love it.

Do you miss dating at all? Do you miss having a lesbian circle?

E: Yes and no. Of course, now I'm in my golden years, so to speak, so I don't really need that anymore. I have my little house and my interest in my pussycats and my books, and also I've had three operations in my life, which I won't go into. I hate old people who talk about their aches and pains. But I had to say bye-bye to a number of little pieces of my anatomy, so I'm not in the running anymore for sex, you know. And I don't miss it because once it happened—and the first thing happened at 42. I had to have a hysterectomy because of some tumors—there went the sex life. And by that time, thank God, I had my little house, and I didn't have to look around for a mate. [*Laughs*]

So I accepted that kind of philosophically, and then along came a couple of other things—that I won't go into here—which further reduced my eligibility for hot sex! And I really didn't give a damn by that time, you know. And to this day I think maybe it was all for the best because I don't have to worry about any little AIDS bugs crawling around in my blood, you know, and I'm sure I would have if I'd stayed whole and healthy. I would have gallivanted around a little too much or something, and I could have easily come by one of those diseases. So, this way I know I'm pretty safe. They say abstinence is the best course, and of course nobody wants to go in for that. But I have, and I'm not sorry. Because, well, after you hit a certain senior age, you don't miss it much, you know?

And who wants to look at you anymore by then, when you're past 60, for God's sake! I mean, you've got wrinkles. You're overweight. One thing or another. And usually, unless you're very lucky, you start having aches and pains and diseases, which I haven't had yet. Nobody looks at you as a love object anymore. And I'm kind of relieved that it's all past, frankly, because I don't have to worry about it anymore.

I have a pretty good life the way things are. I'm not bored. I don't feel frustrated or left out of things. I can be into things just as much as I want to, and I don't want to be. I like it here. People say, "Why don't you go on a cruise around the world? You can afford it. You might *meet* someone!" This is the song and dance I got years ago from the head office girl where I ended up working. And I said, "What do I want to *meet* someone for? I've already got my house. I've already got my life. What do I want some old jerk to louse it up for and maybe claim half of my savings or something!" I said, "I don't care about that!" And she looked at me as though I had two heads or something, but it's true. I don't want anybody around me 24 hours a day. I *love* my friends, but I want them to go home at night, you know? [*Laughs*]

Are your friends mostly gay men and lesbians?

E: Well, as the years go along I find that I don't have too many friends. I have one gay man friend, who lives across the street, incidentally. When they moved in—there were two of them then—I watched them, and I didn't see any women. And I thought, *I bet those two are gay.* So after they'd been there a couple of months, I walked over there one day, and I said, "Hi, welcome. I'm your neighbor from across the street. I see you have a couple of pussycats." They did. So I met the cats. And then, apropos of nothing at all, I said, "You're gay, aren't you?" [*Mimics her neighbors looking stunned*] "Uh." And then I said, "Well, so am I! Hi, neighbor!" And I shook their hands. And they loved that. So every time they went on a trip or something, they'd call and say, "Can you take care of our girls for us?" And that meant the cats. So I would go over and clean the kitty box and feed the cats. And they have special food. And they drink nothing but bottled water. Oh, my. And then every time I needed something done—like change the lightbulb in my kitchen, which has a very high ceiling, and I don't have a tall ladder—I'd call one of the boys over, and they'd climb up the ladder and take that heavy globe thing off, which is too heavy for me anymore, and change the lightbulb for me. And we'd trade back and forth, so it worked out just beautiful.

And then one of the men got cancer of the stomach, and he died. I felt so bad. He looked like he had AIDS, but he didn't. And I just naturally assumed his partner would sell out and move, but he didn't. He's still over there. And he still calls me—"I have to go to Arizona on a business trip. Would you take care of the cats for me?" "Oh, sure!" And I go over and take care of the cats. It works out fine. He saves aluminum cans for me from his office. He brings back a whole big bag of them, and I take them over and get money for them, which helps with the cat food money. And sometimes he mows the strip of lawn in front of my house, which I don't ask him to do, but he does it. He's a real sweetheart. He's a middle-aged guy. You could drive by and wouldn't think twice about him. He's been married and has a child. So far he's been there alone. It's been almost a year now since his partner died. I felt so bad. He was such a nice guy! They both are such swell fellas. I mean, why the hell does that have to happen to people like that? They didn't drink or use drugs or anything like that. And they were real hardworking. They bought that house, and it looks a million times better now than when they got it. The whole place looks so beautiful! And he does it all by himself. I don't know how, but it's just spotless! And I look at this dump, and it's a mess! [*Laughs*] I see him out there shaking the rugs all the time. He's a real housekeeper.

We are so conditioned by our parent culture to want and have a mate, that one person in whom we invest our love and attention. Are you never lonely for this kind of relationship?

E: Well, in the last three alliances I had with girls I would make allowances for things that I really did not admire in them. And after the last one, I thought, *Well, why should I do this for the sake of companionship? What I need to do is to get a place of my own and be my own person, really.* Because I don't want to ally myself with people that I don't really admire.

Earlier you said that you would never have dreamed what would happen in the 70s and 80s—how people would be able to live together openly. It seems that it would have been very difficult to have had a relationship in the 40s and 50s.

E: After my last three short alliances—I never lived with any of them—I was very disappointed in the quality of friends I was finding in those days. I thought, *Well, I think I'll just buy a place of my own and to heck with them.* Around that time, too, I became interested in the Daughters of Bilitis, so I joined them; and that was a nice group of gals, but they mostly were going with somebody else. But I would go to their meetings, and at one of their meetings I met a young lady who had recently come down from out of state. And boy, when she walked by, my eyes went out that far from my head [*holds her hands a foot from her face*]. I thought, *Boy, what a looker!* She was really something.

So I took it upon myself to make her acquaintance and talk to her a little bit during and after the meeting, and she became interested in me. So she came over here—this was after I decided just to cool it—and sure enough, we found a kindred spark. She played guitar and sang, so we got together with our guitars and our singing and other things. Thing is, she lived down in Long Beach, in an apartment there, and she worked down there. She'd come clear up here to see me; we got almost to the serious stage when her company sent her back to where she came from to work at the other office again. And I was heartbroken over this, 'cause I really felt that I would like to live with this person. She said, "Well, we'll see how things are, and maybe you would like to move up here and be with me." And I said, "Yes, I would; I hate my job." She asked me what I really wanted out of life, and I really opened up and told her—I very rarely opened up and told anybody what I wanted out of life. [*Pauses*] And I'm sorry I did because she seemed to accept it at the time, but after she got up there she wrote back and said that she didn't think much of some of the things I wanted out of life. The way she phrased it really cut me to the quick. And about a little less than a month after she moved up there, she met somebody and started living with them. I just about caved in.

So at that stage of the game, I thought, *Well, to hell with gay life.* So I persuaded myself that I hated gays. I cut off all my friends, and I decided I would live here alone. And in fact I wrote a very unfortunate letter to two lady friends of mine, whom I thought the world of, and I said, "Well, I don't like gay life anymore," and I made some horrible remark about the undesirability of gay life and that I wasn't going to be that way anymore or something. I never heard from them again; I don't blame them.

And so, I applied myself to working here, and that was it. I interested myself in folk music and in guitar, and I kept my mind busy. And although I never went nongay, you know, and had a man living here or anything like that, I just quit completely having intimate relations with the ladies. And I got along pretty well that way because I couldn't take anymore of that stuff. I mean, it was just one disappointment after another, and I thought to myself, *Why do I line myself up for it? It isn't worth it. I'm getting along in years; who needs somebody? I've got it all right here. You know, if I just look at the bluebird of happiness in my own yard, I don't really have to dash out to these dives and look for somebody or have somebody come over here that I don't know very well.* You know, who needs it anymore?

Do you think that pain is something that's intrinsic to gay relationships?

E: No, I think that that's bound to come to most people, whether they're gay or heterosexual. I mean, it depends on the person and what they come up with in life. I've seen women who are just as heartbroken over some jerk that they fell for who has left them with a baby they don't want or something. At least I didn't get that. I don't think it really matters.

I think that if you're in for it, you're in for it—no matter if you're nongay or gay. There is a greater chance for it in gay life because of the taboo that we have had to live with for so long. But I think that we have a better chance now that we've come out in the open and society is reluctantly accepting us. I think that people maybe have a better chance of maybe making it than they did in the '40s and '50s because we had to be so secretive about it. So it's a healthier thing now then it was then. I think the more light that we let in, the more chance we have to grow and to have better relationships. But I think that heartbreak comes to lots of people no matter what walk of life they are in.

Of course, I've long ago gotten over this babe. She wrote me a letter once and said, "Well, I'm with so-and-so now, but I'd still like to be friends, and I'd still like to write you letters, and I'd like you to write me letters back." I wrote her one letter back. I said, "Dear so-and-so, I think it's great that you're with another lady now, and since I believe in true and everlasting love between two ladies, I think that if I wrote to you and you wrote to me, it wouldn't be such a good idea. It really wouldn't strengthen your relationship up there, would it? So I'm not going to write to you anymore, but I wish you all the luck in the world." 'Cause I really believe that. I thought, *Now, if I were that girl up there and my gal started writing down here to someone she had had a hot affair with*—which is true—*I wouldn't feel so happy about it, would I?* I mean, just because things didn't work out right for me doesn't give me the right to kind of undermine her relationship up there with somebody else I don't even know. Does it? No, it's not the thing to do.

And that's one thing—as flirtatious as I was, as with-it as I was in my youth, I never got between a girl and her girl. You know what I mean? I never played footsie with somebody who was teamed up with somebody else. I figure what goes on in heterosexual life that way, goes on for us, at least for me, 'cause I have an innate feeling that one should not horse around like that and make people unhappy.

So I've decided to live here by myself. And I'm kind of glad because those surgeries carved me up pretty bad, and I ain't very pretty anymore. I'm not really eligible anymore for romantic love because of this. And so, why try to do it? And then somebody will be repulsed and say, "Oh, my God!" Then I get another hurt heart. So to hell with it. [*Laughs*] That's the way I feel. But I'm in sympathy with all you young gals who are still romantically inclined; I think it's the greatest, you know, but, I just don't want to be with it anymore myself. It's just too much heartbreak.

Muriel W.
San Francisco, California

"*I never lost interest in education,*" *says Muriel W., 74, discussing her devotion to lifelong learning and describing the joy with which she greeted the news in 1943 that she'd earned a full scholarship to attend Brown University in her native Rhode Island.*

"*In high school I could guarantee you that I'd never see the inside of a college. I was just lucky. Oh, I couldn't believe it! The day that you think is the most wonderful day of your life—well, that was it.*"

It is a characteristically damp day in San Francisco when Muriel and I sit down to chat. Her Washington Street flat—which she has occupied for 20 years and shares with her best friend of three decades—is suffocatingly warm, and the air has a stale sickroom quality to it. The vinyl shades in her sitting room are yellow with age and pulled down. The only light comes from a single reading lamp. Stacks of books—from filmographies to tracts of political analysis—line the room. A typewriter and bottles of pills sit on a nearby table, and a small television sits idle in a corner. A photo of President Ronald Reagan stands propped up against a bottle of Kaopectate.

Amid this gloomy setting sits Muriel, bright as a penny and ready for conversation. A recent stroke, which has left her face slightly paralyzed, does not deter her.

"*It's hard to fight the good fight for so long,*" *she says, referring to being gay in a* "*hetero world.*" "*You think sometimes maybe it would have been nice to have had a husband and children and a nice little home, but I obviously didn't want that. If you find yourself in that situation and don't really want it, it can be claustrophobic."*

We look at Muriel's photo albums, which are filled with handsome, 1950s-era Greenwich Village girls wearing harlequin glasses, straight skirts, and car coats.

"All my friends died young," she says ruefully, closing the last album and giving Candy, her 16-year-old Siamese, a gentle pat. "I'd like to show you a picture of my partner and I," she says, "but you can't publish it. She has children, and that would probably make her feel very self-conscious—even though she's dead."

And that does seem to be the unspoken code of many older lesbians, hypervigilant and exceedingly discreet: You can never be too careful.

Muriel has just lost her Catholic Charities caseworker, Maureen Kelly, a hip, kind young woman whom I'd met in a gerontology course at San Francisco State University and through whom I'd been introduced to Muriel. Her new caseworker—an unsympathetic man, according to Muriel—considers her lesbianism an untreated illness.

"I imagine he thinks I have psychological problems," says Muriel, both saddened and amused by her dilemma. "But I just want companionship, someone to talk with. That's what Maureen used to do—just talk to me and be my friend. I wonder if the people who study geriatrics know that's all we need."

Interviewed July 1986

Being a Sinner Takes a Certain Vitality

I'll bet there were very few women on the Brown campus at the time of your admission.

M: There were no women faculty.

And students?

M: There were 100 students at Pembroke, which was a separate section for the girls. In those days it was like Harvard. Brown University already existed, but when they started admitting girls, they admitted them to a college in the university called Pembroke. But then you took your courses mostly on the men's campus. If you wanted to study certain subjects, you got the same lectures that the men received. My attending college was unusual in the sense that not many people could afford to go, but it wasn't so unusual that I was a woman.

In fact, that's one thing that probably would be interesting to know—in the 1930s and '40s I never felt any discrimination against me because I was a girl or because I wanted to do something that mostly men did. I was accepted as if I were a man and wanted to do this. And most of my friends at Pembroke who were dedicated students and got scholarships felt the same way. And I found that we lived on a fairly high intellectual level in the sense that we were interested in current affairs and what was going on then. That was the beginning of liberalism—under Roosevelt, you know—and we really believed in that. Everybody had a right to speak and the right to his own opinion. For example, my costudents would never dream of trying to get a speaker off the stage who was invited by the college to speak, even though they didn't like his or her politics. We would consider that not only wrong but bad manners. We took it seriously. We lived in a country where everyone had a right to his or her own opinion. At that time a lot of the people in government or in institutions or in business were conservative. And we most likely disagreed with them, but we certainly believed they had a right to come and be heard. It was a great time because we were living the ideal of Americanism at that point.

And I met a girl there who was terribly interesting. She was so interesting that I took all of the rest of my seminars with her. I learned so much with her, through her. Her research was done very thoroughly. Her mother had been a feminist of the '20s and before. And we became very good friends.

Did you know you were gay at this point?

M: No. [*Laughs*] It's just so funny. Well, I think it's funny because it never even occurred to me. I knew that I was very attracted to women, and I liked their friendship. And I got more satisfaction, it seemed to me, out of the friendships I had with them than I had with just a date with a boy, although I was very attracted to boys at the time too. I had the usual dates, and I assumed I'd get married sometime, but I never really thought that much about it. It was sort of an idea way in the future.

I became engaged while I was in college. Then the boy broke the engagement. I think I was really in love with him. He was the only male person I've ever felt that way about—the way I have felt about girls. But no, I never heard much about lesbianism at that time. It was never mentioned or talked about. There may have been gay girls around me, but I didn't know if they were. No one ever said. I did hear rumors about a very wealthy girl at the college who had a girlfriend who lived off campus. And I wondered why the girlfriend would bother to come up to Providence just to be with her friend. I mean, it didn't seem to be done, ordinarily. Later on, I gathered that they were lovers. They were discreet about it, so no one said anything about it or mentioned it much. Well, they lived in a group of their own. They were very wealthy people. I won't say that they didn't bother with others; they just had different standards by which they lived. And we all thought they were just out of our reach. We just didn't bother, and so they never bothered much with us. I guess we thought they were pretty—what's the word? Fast! That was it. They had standards about living that we middle-class people didn't accept.

And I remember one girl missing a semester. And a friend of mine said, "Oh, I bet Skylar"—her name was Skylar Murphy—"got pregnant." And I said, "She won't be coming back?" And she said, "Oh, no, she'll be coming back." And I said, "Isn't she going to get married to the person, whoever he might be, if she is pregnant?" My friend was more sophisticated than I was. [*Laughs*] And she said, "No, I guess she wanted a tumble in the hay, and certainly her family wouldn't want her to marry him." And I thought, *How strange. My family would have found it an absolute necessity for me to marry him.* [*Laughs*]

At any rate, that was my first introduction to any kind of thought about sexual matters that was beyond the conventional idea. But no, lesbianism never occurred to me. I couldn't even imagine how you did it if you were in love with a girl. [*Laughs*] All I knew was I had a lot of very close friendships.

And so, as I said, I became engaged to this young man. And I really intended to marry him, although I knew he wouldn't be accepted by my mother because he was a different religion. It would be the same thing [as my parents' marriage] all over again—a Catholic and a Protestant.

It's so funny to hear that now. It doesn't seem such a big deal to be a Catholic with a Protestant.

M: I guess it isn't now, but it was then. Especially in New England, and especially among Irish Catholics. My mother, I guess, had had a hard time growing up in New England because so many of the older settlers were English Protestants. In fact, in newspapers you would read a job listed, and at the end of the listing it would say: "No Catholics, No Irish Need Apply."

Really?

M: I'm not exaggerating. You were allowed not to want to have an Irish Catholic working for you or anything like that. Does it sound as if I come from the Middle Ages somehow? [*Laughs*]

Of course, I was brought up with the usual prejudice. My mother thought that anyone who wasn't a Catholic was not as good as she was. You know. I'd hear people talk about Jews, and she didn't particularly like Jews either. I'm afraid my mother didn't particularly like anybody except her own kind. [*Laughs*]

I remember going to high school. The first person that I became close friends with was named Mildred. We'd get there early to meet so we could take a walk around school before classes. And then early in the year—because it was the fall—she wasn't there for a couple of days. And I said, "Where's Millie?" And they said, "Oh, she's off because of the Jewish holidays." And I said, "She's Jewish?" And they said, "Yes, didn't you know?" And I said, "No." And then I thought to myself that all the things that people say about other races or groups of people is hogwash because she was just like me, I felt. We had the same ideas and the same things in common, so I immediately lost my prejudice or feelings of estrangement from other people. The lesson came very fast. Well now, I guess we should get down to fundamentals because all I seem to be talking about is background.

That's OK. It's all integral. Now, what would you consider a fundamental?

M: Well, when I discovered I was gay, I guess, would be a fundamental. My mother was very, very strict about sex particularly, you know. She was always so very domineering and possessive, which is understandable in some ways, but it's hard to live with. And she was always accusing me of some horrible sexual thing that I was [supposedly] doing that I'd never even heard of before. [*Laughs*]

What did she accuse you of?

M: She would say to me, "Why do you spend so much time in Jocelyn's room?" Jocelyn was an out-of-town girl, one of my best friends at college. I didn't know what my mother meant. I mean, what was wrong with seeing a girl in her room? I wasn't seeing a boy in his room, which I could understand my mother would object to. It never occurred to me that she'd ever heard of homosexuality or anything. And I would get very upset, you know. "What's the trouble? Why shouldn't I see her or spend time with her if I like her? She's a friend of mine." And this put thoughts in my head. Or she'd mention details, you now—did I do this or that with my boyfriend on a date? And I didn't even know that one *could* do this or that on a date—or that one *did*. [*Laughs*] I think parents sometimes put ideas in kids' heads, if they don't have them already.

I was very—as you can gather—very naive sexually when I was growing up. I didn't know anything about anything. I mean, I hadn't had any sex at all by the time I graduated college. I guess that's another thing that seems strange to the younger generation. But even with my boyfriend when I was engaged to him, I still thought that you should wait till you got married. He accepted that. I mean, the boy did accept that, if that's what you promoted. So, when [my boyfriend broke our engagement], it really hit me hard. I was in my last year at college, and I didn't do very well, I'm afraid. My marks went down. I skipped classes. I just didn't have the will to do anything.

Did anyone inquire? It would seem a rather dramatic departure to go from being an honors student to being a slacker in a single semester.

M: Yes. The dean called me into her office. I assumed at that time that people in authority wouldn't understand my problems. I guess that's a young person's feeling at all times. And so I put a good face on it and went in—appearing, I hoped, my usual, efficient self. And she asked me what was the matter, and I said, "Nothing." And she said, "Well, do you have anything upsetting you in your home life or in your private life, like a broken engagement?" Probably the rumors had gone around by that time through the campus. And I said, "Oh, no, no, no. I'm perfectly all right." And she said, "Well, knowing your past record, I suggest that you get to some classes and do the work that's required and get it in on time." And so I said I certainly would and thanked her for her interest, and I left. And that was that. I was used to trying to put on a good face. That's how one was brought up then. I don't think she could have helped even if I had told her what was wrong because the main thing [that was wrong] was at home. My mother got more and more possessive as I got more and more independent because I seemed to grow away from her as I got older. I was close to a nervous breakdown. I know that.

It's interesting; I met a priest up there at Brown. He was a student, a graduate student. And Jack—a boy that I had known for years, who was like a brother—and I had marvelous discussions with him. I like friendships with men—they're fun, there's a difference in the way their minds work, and there's a vitality about them. And one evening at dinner I started to talk a bit about [my life at home]. And the priest said, "I think you should do something. I don't think you should stay there. You'll withdraw so far into yourself," he said, "that it may take years for you to come back." And that had a powerful effect on me.

So I decided I would leave home. And I told Jack about it, and Jack told my girlfriend Peggy, and she said, "Well, come stay with me." She had a duplex apartment in a nice neighborhood in New York. Her father was wealthy. And Jocelyn, my best friend, encouraged me to leave also, and we had a discussion about it. So I had quite a bit of support in that way, and I decided to leave home on the day I graduated, which made a very dramatic graduation. My friend Peggy said, "Why don't you just say that you're coming to stay as a guest for a couple of weeks after graduation." I said, "I can't tell my mother I'm doing anything. She would never permit it. If possible, she'd probably lock the door and not let me get out until graduation."

So I just pretended that nothing was going on. I couldn't take any clothes with me or anything like that because my mother would see me packing a bag, so I just went to graduation exercises and went through them. And Jocelyn offered to lend me money. In those days things were so cheap, and she said she could spare, say, from $20 to $50. And I said, "Gee, I don't know." So she said, "All right. Whatever you think you need." So I borrowed $20 from her, so I could buy a couple of pieces of clothing. I had dressed up for graduation and worn a dress underneath my cap and gown. So I couldn't tell my mother I was going to New York with Peggy, who was also *Jewish.*

Even worse!

M: Yes, worse crimes! At the graduation [my mother] said, "Why don't we all have lunch together?"—meaning my aunt and myself. And I told her then that I had a date to see Jocelyn and have lunch with her and her husband. It was the best excuse I could think of. I said, "I'm not going to be seeing them again because they're leaving town." And she said, "Well, all right. Don't be too late when you come home."

So, I did a little shopping and grabbed myself a bite of lunch, and then I met Peggy's parents, the Levys, at the train station at a quarter to four. It was a 4 o'clock train from Providence to New York. Her father had already bought the tickets, and I thought, *Oh, thank heavens! I have another $4 left to do something with!* [*Laughs*] What small sums we had to work with in those days. And I was still worried; I was worried about my mother all this time because I knew how upset she'd be when I didn't come home.

Did you call her when you arrived in New York?

M: No, I sent her a telegram. I just wanted her to know where I was. I wrote her a letter the next day and sent it special delivery, explaining why I had to leave home. I thought she might be able to read this. Whenever we started to discuss anything, we got into such fights. I'd get wound up and say things that she didn't like, and she'd say things that would upset me, and we never got anywhere.

So I thought if I wrote it all down on paper, she would have to read it—somewhere, quietly—and not be able to answer back until I got the whole thing out. And I thought she might begin to understand then, but she didn't. She just wrote me a letter saying, "I will send you a ticket back to Providence, and I want you here on such-and-such a day and such-and-such a time." And she said, "You've had your fun. You've seen the big city, but you'd better come home now." She implied that she'd try to prosecute me in some way.

How old were you?

M: I was 19. So I told Mr. Levy, who was a lawyer, what had happened, and I asked him what I should do. And he said that in New York you are of legal age at 18. So, he said, "If your mother wants you back home, and you don't want to go back home, the only way that she can get you to go back home is to get you extradited from New York to Rhode Island." And he said, "It'll cost her some money." And I thought to myself, *She's not going to pay the money.* I didn't think she had it, anyway, to pay. And I didn't think she'd go that far with it. She was always threatening things, you know, but never intended to carry them out.

But everything worked out pretty well then. And Mr. Levy got me a job. His sister was personnel manager at an insurance company, so I think what he did was to call up and say, "Listen, I got a gal here who's staying with my daughter, and she needs a job. Get her anything." For all I know, he said, "Get her out of my hair!" But, no, he seemed very nice. In fact, he loaned me $20 while I was there without even asking me if I needed it. I found it under my bag when I went up to the room I was sharing with Peg. He thought I needed more money. At that point I did.

So then I took the job, and that's where I met Maggie, my roommate. She was hired a couple months later, and we got to be friends. She was also a very unusual person, I thought. I mean different, not run-of-the-mill. I didn't like conventional people. I liked people who were different. The company had a cafeteria up on the top floor, and she'd bring a book of Latin poetry to read during lunch. That was not what the usual typist did on lunch hour. [*Laughs*] And I noticed it one day, passing by. I could never resist knowing what books people are reading. I thought, *Well, what is she doing here? Why is she working in a place like this?* So I went over to her table one day, sat down, and I said, "Do you mind if I join you?" And she said, "No." So we started talking, and then we became friends. I've known her ever since, and that's since 1943. That's a long time to be friends—and *just* friends; that's all we've ever been. At that point I wasn't thinking of anything else.

And, as I said, I think I was having a nervous breakdown then. I felt different. I can't explain in what way, but I knew something was happening to me. And I began to drink because it seemed I felt less guilty about leaving home after I had a couple of drinks, and I also seemed to feel able to pull myself together and get things done better when I had some liquor in me. And so that went on. It was the social thing to do, it was acceptable. And during the war everyone drank like a fish. In New York anyway. I mean, everyone you'd meet [would say], "Let's go have a drink." So naturally I became an alcoholic. I say "naturally" because that's the usual sequence, isn't it? [*Laughs*] But, no, it did help me escape at the time. And I was very upset about not being able to go on to graduate school. I was offered a teaching fellowship at Brown. It didn't pay enough money for me to be able to live on my own and still go to school and pay rent and buy food and buy books, and so I couldn't take it. That, I think, probably bothered me more than anything else. There it was, right there, and I couldn't live at home. Obviously, by then, if I'd gone back, it would have been worse. I also don't think I could have done the work at that time.

So then I went on getting jobs. I worked with civil service mainly during the war, in personnel, which paid well. Of course, being young, I had dates with young men and so forth. And I still wasn't, I mean, thinking of anything else but perhaps meeting another man like the boy I knew and had been engaged to. I never met one that I thought I could feel the same way about, and I was beginning to get angry with men because I thought the way they treated women was not terribly attractive. You know, they're just interested in sex, and they take you on a date.

So, I decided I would have my [first] sexual experience. Before the war ended or before I was 21, I was going to have sex with somebody. It was one of those things. I had decided I wasn't going to die a virgin. [*Laughs*] I think that was probably because of the psychology books that were coming out then.

What did they say?

M: Oh, that sex was a natural part of life, which it is, but if you don't have it, you're repressed and neurotic and unattractive. So anyway, it was a kind of a pressure, you know. Here all my girl-friends, close friends I knew, were getting married. It was a time when girls did get married when they first graduated from college. The war was on. Of course people were getting married quickly because the men were going overseas. I felt like a jerk. [*Laughs*] You know, I didn't have a particular boyfriend or anything.

Anyway, I met a Frenchman, and I asked him if he'd go to bed with me. [*Laughs*] He was working in a civil service job, and I could tell he was attracted to me. And so one day we got talking, and I asked him if he'd like to go to bed with me. It was definitely not done in those days! He looked at me sort of surprised, and he said, "Oh, that would be very nice! When shall we do it?" [*Laughs*] So I explained to him that I was a virgin, so he wouldn't be disappointed. This I picked up somewhere—if men were going to go to bed with somebody they were not going to marry, they wanted to have a good time. Well, I wasn't experienced enough to give him a good time, but I wanted him to do something for me. And that was really the point.

So we went out, and I had a lot to drink, and we had dinner, and then I took him back to my room, and we went to bed. And I thought, *Oh, is that what sex is?* It was all over. I couldn't believe it was so simple a process! And I thought, *Why is everyone making such a fuss over it?* [*Laughs*]

So, after that I guess I felt a little bit better. And I occasional-ly had a boyfriend, and after he'd leave I'd think, *Well, at least I'm*

*doing what I should be doing. I'm supposed to be having a good time,
so I had a good time, and I am being normal.* I don't know about this
emphasis on being "normal"; maybe it was in the back of my
mind that there were other pressures coming forth. But it seemed
the more I went to bed with a man, the more I became interested in women.

So I thought maybe I could work it out this way—I could have
very close women friends and be married to a man, which would
be conventional enough. Then I went to Europe, and my perspective changed on a number of things. And I didn't want to
come back to New York, but I did.

Was the war on in Europe?

M: No, this is later. This is 1951. The war was over then. Europe,
however, was quite interesting—the result of the war, you know.
England was busily building London up, great activity. Paris was
in the doldrums. I think one building I saw construction workers
working on. Course, they hadn't been bombed so much; they had
been occupied, which I suppose is a different type of psychological scar. But I liked Paris. I got a different perspective on me. I
was defined in a way that I didn't expect I would be, you know.
I guess when you come up against a different culture, it does that.

What do you think happened to you in those ten weeks?

M: Well, one thing—I went over with the idea that I was going to
stay there. And I visited this young man I'd been corresponding
with and I'd met here during the war. I thought that I might stay
and marry him, and he asked me to marry him. And then, meantime, I had been corresponding with a British girl. She lived outside of London, in a small place outside of Portsmouth. And
[when I arrived] I went to visit her, and I guess I fell in love with
her. And it was something that made me realize that I couldn't do

what I'd been planning to do all the time—get my pleasurable contacts, my emotional contacts, from women, as I said, and marry a man and have children and have a conventional position in life. I realized it wasn't going to work out that way because I enjoyed being with her so much more than I enjoyed being with him. I wouldn't have wanted to spend even a couple of hours with him if I were married to him. It wasn't that he was unpleasant; he was a very polite, stuffy Englishman. He didn't have the sex appeal that my boyfriend in college had, so that was not there. I wasn't even attracted to him. So I came back here, and maybe that's what did it. Maybe everything blew up.

Did anything happen with this woman? Did she know how you felt?

M: I don't know. I think she felt the same way, but I don't think she was ready to say so. She was seeing a boy, and she stopped seeing him when I was there, and he said something to her, and she said, "I'd much rather be with Muriel." And that was the way I felt about her—I'd much rather see her than go out with Derrick, the young man in London.

But that's as far as it ever got. We planned to go to a small town in England and stay in a little inn, but I never got around to it. My money gave out, and I had to go home. I hadn't even admitted anything yet; I just realized that this particular plan that I was forming in my mind wasn't going to work.

How old were you when you were there?

M: I was 28 when I went over.

And so you came back to quite a different world.

M: Yeah. It did seem very different to me, every aspect of it. And I got very sick, so it was hard for me to go to work. I got a job, finally, and then I went to a psychiatrist. And the first thing I wanted to talk about was whether or not I was a lesbian.

Did you have that vocabulary?

M: No, I said I thought I might be a *homosexual.* I didn't even know that "homosexual" didn't apply to women. I thought anyone who liked the same sex was a homosexual. He said, "Oh, don't talk nonsense! You're no homosexual." And so I thought, *That's a big help. That's the one thing I wanted to talk about. [Laughs]*

What did you talk about then?

M: I guess I talked about my childhood. I guess he wanted to see what kinds of problems were hidden in my childhood. And, I don't know, maybe what I became was caused by my childhood. I have no idea.

Then I broke out in a rash. I'd been given to having eczema as a child, and I still have it. Whenever I got nervous I'd break out all over my face and my hands and my arms, my breasts and my body. And I had asthma. And I had it so badly that at times I couldn't even sleep. I was a mess. And a friend of mine, an Armenian girl I went to college with, who was living in New York at the time, said she'd take me to a doctor. And her family paid the bill, which was nice.

Were you still drinking?

M: No, I wasn't able to. I didn't want to. It was probably the liquor that destroyed my nerves, and it didn't help any after a while. I was living with Maggie at the time, and so she paid the rent—and quite graciously, without any comment or criticism about it. And she bought the food, which was all I needed at that point. I wasn't thinking beyond. I had left everything behind me, and I could just focus on one simple matter of eating and having a place to sleep, and that's all I focused on. And she did the rest. She went to work, and I usually cooked because she hates to cook, and so I had some little thing fixed for her when she got home. And I read a lot at that point, in a calmer frame of mind, and I started to write a little bit. I had always wanted to write, and I thought I'd write down my thoughts. And as I wrote, it was amazing what came up through the process of trying to dig deeply. Even a choice of words or a phrase—suddenly you realize this has more than a symbolic meaning. There's something there. I talked about not being able to breathe because I'd been so oppressed. Then one night I dreamt about the girl who had taken me to the doctor. I dreamt that we were having sex.

And I woke up in the morning, and I thought, *My God, I'm a homosexual. I'm a lesbian.* Then I accepted the fact. And I thought, *The next affair I have is going to be with a woman, for sure.* That's when I realized. And I thought, *Well, I'll look this over for a bit and not make any hasty judgment of the dream I had,* because the psychiatrist had taught me a little bit about dreams—that they could mean other things.

So, I got some books, and every damn psychology book I picked up always said that homosexuals were sick. And I thought, *I don't want to be sick. I want to be normal.* I didn't like that explanation. But I knew that my feelings made me feel good, so I decided to ignore the psychology books.

A wise decision.

M: And then I began to feel very well—all put together in one piece, an integrated personality. I don't know how it happened. I can't tell anybody how it happened. It just happened. Then I decided that I wanted to go back to work, and I wanted to get things done. My doctor said to wait a couple of weeks, but I was tired of hanging around. I really didn't want to live on Maggie; it wasn't fair to her. But the point was, for the first time in my life I had relaxed. She was doing all this for me, and I didn't feel an undue obligation, and never did she make me feel that way. So I thought that I should be out working. I mean, who wants to sit around doing nothing? So then I went looking for a job. And it was amazing the amount of self-confidence that I had. I wasn't afraid of anything. If I didn't get the job, I thought to myself, *Well, I probably didn't want it.* I went down to apply for unemployment insurance, and that gave me a bit of money coming in. So I wasn't worried. I felt very relaxed. I thought no one could ever do anything to me again and harm me. I guess it doesn't hurt any-one to go through a phase like that.

So, I got a job in offset printing at an engineering consultant company whose offices were at Rockefeller Center in New York, and that's where I met Marion.

The boss woman who hired me was at my desk, telling me how to set things up, and the phone rang, and she had to go, and she sent Marion over to help me. And Marion came over, and we looked at each other, and there was an instant recognition. I don't know either how that happens, but she said, "I'm so-and-so," and I told her, "I'm so-and-so," and we shook hands very formally. But I thought to myself, *I'm going to be a friend of hers for the rest of my life.* That's the kind of thing that you can't explain, but it hap-pened that way. And we found we were very compatible in our ideas. She was a musician and was just taking this job to tide her over until she got another job in music.

I was really fascinated by this woman. She was 12 years older than I was, and I was interested in the fact that she played the harp. It was an unusual instrument to play, and she was good too. She had been a child prodigy. She'd had a scholarship to Curtis Institute in Philadelphia at the age of 12. And she was playing with Stokowski's orchestra at the age of 12. And she had so much vitality! She had the vitality of three people put together. And I didn't have too much vitality at that point. I was getting it—it was coming back—and then I began to have more than I'd ever had! I realized that what had been eating away at my energy was what was going on in my head, the guilt and the worry about home—of course, the drinking didn't help, and my nerves didn't help, and not feeling like a whole person didn't help.

And then the more I saw Marion, the more I liked her. And then I fell in love with her. I didn't know what to do about that! [*Laughs*] I was at least able to admit it to myself—"I'm in love with this woman"—and not to be afraid of it, recognizing it, admitting it. I just wondered what she thought about the idea. I didn't say anything.

I went on enjoying her company, and then I would stay over on weekends sometimes. We enjoyed each other's company so much that she thought it would be better if I stayed over. We wouldn't have to bother coming back and forth, you now. We lived quite a ways away in New York. And so one night I decided, *This has got to go somewhere. It can't just stop here.* And so I was plotting my little plots. And one night, a Saturday night, I stayed over, and the lights were out, and I thought, *I've got to do something about this.* I was getting too nervous about the way things were going—*weren't* going, I should say. [*Laughs*]

So, I made some excuse about getting up to get some water, and I had to pass by her bedside. And coming back, I went over to her bed and asked her if I could kiss her good night, and she instantly recognized what I had in mind. And I could also feel her body stiffen with tension at the fact that she wanted and was thinking the same thing. So I kissed her, and then I stopped. I didn't know where to go next. She said, "Do whatever you want to do. I'm 1,000% sensual." And I said [plaintively], "I don't know what to do." And she said, "I thought you were experienced." [*Laughs*] And I said, "No." She said, "You've never known another woman before?" I said, "No." And she said, "Well, come on to bed."

She had "known" women?

M: Yes. She was very experienced. She was a wonderful person. She knew so much about the psychology of sex and the spirituality of sex and what it meant between two people, and I learned all of this from her. I never realized what it was all about, and then I suddenly began to realize what it was all about.

When Marion said, "Come to bed," did that surprise you?

M: No. I kind of thought that she might say that. But it surprised me that she first wanted to make sure that I wanted to go to bed with a woman. You know, she said, "Maybe you're lonely and needing sex, and you're just using me instead of a man." And I said no, that wasn't true at all. I said, "I thought you would have known by now that I'm in love with you." And she said she had a lot of obligations in her own life, and she didn't think she was a very stable person to be in love with. And I said it didn't matter. No matter what happened in the future, I didn't care. I was in love with her, and I wanted her. I seemed to convince her.

So I guess I was able to give myself 100%. It was a total giving in, a total trust also. I never trusted anyone else that much before. It was kind of like a little miracle happening.

That miracle came out of your decision to be yourself.

M: Yes. I think what is important is that even if a person needs something, she has to be in good condition for it to work. Sometimes I had met people I loved, and I don't think it would have worked out because I needed them, but it was about dependence. When my life began to come together, I felt only then could I give myself 100% to this relationship. She was in the same situation too. She had been an alcoholic too, and had become a member of a 12-step program a couple of years before. That's how I got into recovery, through her. I thought it would help to bring us together, which it did. So then I moved in with her, but

I continued to pay half my rent to Maggie. I couldn't leave her holding the bag like that, after she'd done so much for me.

When I told Maggie that I was a lesbian, she said, "Oh, I always thought so." I said, "Why didn't you tell *me*!" And she said, "Well, I thought you should find out by yourself." Maybe she was right.

It's often the case that people know before we do.

M: Yes. And Marion liked Maggie very much. I said to Maggie, "I thought you'd object." And she said, "You mean, I'd pull my skirts aside when you passed by?" And I said, "Something like that." She is a very tolerant person. She accepts people as they are. So we stayed friends all that time.

Marion and I lived together from September 19, 1953—I remember that date as if I had gotten married. Well, that's the way I felt—I was truly married. I remember saying something one day about running into someone who'd just gotten married, and Marion felt upset because she was keeping me from getting married. And I said, "What are you talking about? I *am* married. To you. What's the difference?" She had two children, which was the difference in her point of view.

She'd been married previously?

M: Yeah. And she had lived in a small town in Pennsylvania. And of course she was afraid of people knowing. And this fear of people knowing can make things difficult.

What was that like, being a lesbian couple in the 1950s? When I think 1950s, I think witch-hunts.

M: I don't think of it that way. I always felt free to do what I thought. I think I was pretty independent. I did what I liked, and I didn't have anyone to answer to. I've heard it said that San Francisco is the capital of homosexuality, but I found it much freer in New York. New Yorkers don't seem to care about what you do, as long as you don't talk about it too much. [*Laughs*] If you're discreet—I think that was the thing that was indicative of the '50s. I didn't mind that. I knew there was going to be a little difficulty, but I never suffered from it. And even though people might have known about it or suspected, they never treated me any differently, as long as I wasn't blatant about it.

And I think that's what people object to—if they disapprove of something, and you're blatant about it, sort of trying to make them feel that they're stupid because they don't approve of you. And I think everyone has the right to their particular belief. If you don't want to be a lesbian, OK, don't be one. Why should you be? If they leave me alone, I leave them alone. And I found that with people whom I was really friends with, I told them, and they never made a fuss about it. They invited Marion along anytime they invited me somewhere. So, I never had any particular unpleasantness occur.

But as I said, every time I would pick up a damn psychology book it would say the same thing—"The homosexual is highly neurotic and sick." These were the liberals. They thought they were being very tolerant. You asked me what it was like in the '50s—liberals thought they were being very tolerant and understanding by saying the person is sick and neurotic, and we have to be kind to them. [*Laughs*] One time a friend of mine, whom I liked very much, said something like that. And I said, "They're not sick." And he said, "Well I thought it was more understanding to say they were disturbed than to criticize them as sinful, as the church would say." I said, "I would rather be considered a sinner than a sick person. Saying we're sick takes away a person's dignity." I guess it's a way of saying that it's not your fault. You know, you get pneumonia, it's not your fault. But if you're a sinner, that requires a certain amount of vitality and independence of spirit! So I'd rather have the church's definition of it, if I'm going to be anything. I can't believe it's a sin. Nor could Marion. She said anything that beautiful that could exist between two people could never be considered a sin by a God who talked of the spirit of love. And that's the way I thought.

At least now there are visible groups of us, and there is a language, and there is an understanding and a body of literature; and it seems that it would have been enormously difficult 30 years ago without a culture.

M: There was a subculture—quite sub. For me it was quite sub. I met [other lesbians] in the 12-step group. Some girls would even go so far as not to shop anywhere that wasn't run by a gay person, whether a gay man or a gay woman. And I thought that was going too far. I mean, I accepted [it], but I didn't agree with it.

And then there was the culture of the bars. You know, that's where you met, of course. It was a very in thing. And I think in some way we probably enjoyed it because there were phrases and words that we used that were very in—among lesbians, you know—but the rest of the world didn't know about them.

Almost a secret language. Can you recall some of it?

M: Not a lot. I met a girl who told me that they had a word for a woman who had been a lesbian who went with men or was bisexual. Of course, they had a term for the girls who were masculine. I guess the gay world had been patterned after the heterosexual world—the masculine types and the feminine types, you know, the femmes and the butches. And that sort of thing.

Was the gay subculture truly patterned in that way, or was that just the popular view?

M: No, it was. Many of the older women I knew—I mean, my own age at the time—[were butch and femme]. At that time I thought

I should look more masculine than I did if I were going to be a lesbian. And I couldn't understand why I didn't look that way. And in the bars, particularly, the girls were quite divided, the butches and the femmes. And the butches, of course, were not interested in other butches; they were interested in femmes. And then a friend told me about the term "kiki," which was a woman who was both and neither. And this girl was very scornful of these people. In her mind, you had to be all one or all the other—to be accepted by her anyway. It was role-playing to a certain extent.

Was that a class phenomenon, or would you say it was widespread throughout the gay community?

M: I think it was probably more widespread among the lower classes. I met a girl who came to work where I was, and she was from a poor Italian family, and her parents didn't know what was going on. She had a whole set of clothing that she wore when she went out—she was dressed in drag, practically—and she was a butch. And she had a girlfriend who was very, very feminine-looking, as feminine as anybody could get, in looks at least. A friend of mine, a gay man who I worked with, said, "Maybe we should take her out." Because she seemed to be so very unhappy about her situation. Talk to her, make her feel better. Eventually we did. We went to a gay bar, and I talked about how not to feel so upset about it. Her parents couldn't possibly understand, and she shouldn't expect them to. To forget about them, in a sense, and try to come to terms with what she wants and not to let it bother her so much. I guess she was a pretty neurotic person. Course, the boys at work made fun of her all the time. She was very, very butch looking, you know. A lot of fellows in the packing room of the production department weren't terribly educated, and they would see a girl like her, and they'd make fun of her. A couple of times I told them to let her lead her own way of life;

they didn't have to take part in it. I don't now if it helped or not. But I know that when I was in that 12-step program there were a lot of gay people in the Village groups, and when I started to identify myself they would call me when some gay girl went off the wagon or was having trouble making it. I liked doing it. I enjoyed doing it. I felt so good about myself that I wanted everyone else to. I would try to tell them that no matter how bad life seemed, if you get through this situation, you can get through anything. You don't let it bother you. And I was grateful that I had a place to go to keep me from drinking. I had stopped before, but now I had something solid to hold on to. And it helped doing this kind of work. So I had a chance there to talk to some gay girls.

I personally don't think I could have stayed sober if I hadn't come out of the closet, so to speak. The girls thought that they were drinking so much because they *were* out of the closet, and I don't think so. Anyway, it was just what I needed to become a complete and whole person. And to be able to feel so much love for another person seemed to inspire me to feel this overflow towards other people. I wouldn't say I loved them, but I had concern for them. I mean genuine concern and compassion for what happened to them.

And a couple of times I think I did help one of the gay girls. One of them was living at home with her mother, and she only existed in gay groups. She worked in a gay bar. She dressed like a man and so forth. She was always having trouble with her mother, always fighting. And she was quite violent herself. And she seemed to take a shine to me; I met her at a meeting. I never spoke to her because she seemed sort of pathetic in a way, not responding to what people said. So I guess because I showed some interest, she wouldn't let me go. I would tell her about my experiences at home and my mother, how you can overcome that kind of thing. I told her that I thought if she stopped existing only in the gay world, working in a gay bar, and living in drag all the time, that if she dressed normally, like a woman, she could get a better job, and that might help her.

Did she do that?

M: Yes, she did. She went to computer school. They weren't called computers then. They were in the accounting department. Oh, yes, key punching. She learned how to become a keypunch programmer, and she worked her way up. I don't know what happened to her; we didn't keep in touch. I introduced her to other girls in the group, and especially one who was very bright and studying to be a doctor. I thought it would be better for this first girl to meet, shall we say, some higher types, more intelligent types, because she just felt so down and was living on the dregs of society—not the gay bars, not people who were gay, but I mean people who got drunk, you know, and that sort of thing. To be around that all the time is not terribly wholesome or healthful. And to know that this other girl was gay also and was studying to become a doctor, I thought, would make her feel better. Here were some people who have talent, and who are intelligent, and who are going into professions, and they're gay, and they're not worried about it, and they accept it, and they like it and so on. I thought it would be helpful to her.

And then Marion and I broke up.

We got back together about three times. [*Laughs*] I guess it was something we had that we couldn't let go. We broke up the first time because she was given a job in *The King and I*, playing the harp, and so she went on the road tour of the show. Marion called me and told me about this offer, and I said, "Well, is this the opportunity you've been waiting for?" And she said, "Well, it means that I'll have to go on tour for a year and a half with the show." And I said, "Well, I don't like that very much, but you have to go."

I, myself, had to learn the discipline of not being so possessive. I guess I had fallen in my mother's trap because that was one of my faults. With people I liked I got very possessive of them, and I didn't want them, of course, to do anything that would pull them away from me. And so I said, "Well, we'll have to face that when we come to it—but take the part." And she was, of course, very happy. This is what she wanted, and of course she was getting paid very well for it, which was also nice. Because she always worried about her children. She wasn't supporting them; their father was. They were living at home with their father.

And of course they had no idea that their mother was a lesbian.

M: No. I think that her first son suspected something. He was a pretty savvy guy. I went to stay with them one Christmas—or New Year's, it was. I think he saw us kissing in the hallway, and I always suspected that he knew. But the younger son was very jealous of her. I think he would have been very jealous if he had known.

So, anyway, to make a long story short, we were broken up by a woman who was, I think, interested in Marion, but she was not a practicing lesbian. I think she probably had all the instincts for it but never allowed herself to admit them or to do anything about it. Anyway, when Marion came back she moved in with this woman. They bought a house together, as a matter of fact.

Wow! I'll bet you were surprised.

M: Well, I knew about it when I went on my vacation. I got my vacation so I could go out and spend it with Marion. She was out here in California on tour. And she told me.

Something didn't strike me as right about this. Of course, Marion was always sensitive to public opinion. We're talking about public pressure, public opinion. I think it was because of her children. Because if she'd had just herself to worry about, I don't think it would have mattered. But I think this other woman, who came from New England, from the ruling upper-class types, I think she used a kind of moral blackmail on Marion. When Marion went back to New York we were going to get a larger apartment together because where I was living was quite small. And I think this woman told her how unfair this would be to Marion's children, that she would be neglecting them, you know, and that she [the New England woman] could afford to buy a house. And she wanted Marion to come with her and bring her children, and then Marion wouldn't have anything to worry about. I think Marion, in her own mind, thought this woman was not gay and that people couldn't accuse them of being gay if she lived with this woman.

When I went out to see her in California, she was very different. She said, "I can't [move in with you]. You must be stupid to think I could do it with you! Everybody would know!" I said, "The one profession you're in is the one profession that is most tolerant of gay people—the theater!" But she went to live with her. [*Laughs*]

How long did that last?

M: About two years. Of course, at first I was angry. And then I began to try to analyze what was going on there. The funny thing is, even though she went to live with this woman, I knew that she was in love with me and that, given other circumstances, she probably would have come back to me.

So about three years later she called me up. I was still in the same apartment, and she asked me if she could come over. She was in another play, an off-Broadway musical, and she was right close by where I lived down in the Village. At first I was wondering, *What's she going to do now that is going to upset my life?* And then I thought, *Well, I have to see her if she wants to see me.* I couldn't refuse. So I said, "Sure, come on over." We didn't talk very much then, but she told me that she was back playing the harp again. She had quit playing when she was with this woman. I don't know why. It seemed to have a corroding effect on her creativity. She always stopped playing when this woman was in her life, it seemed. And she said, "It's been far too long since I've played, and it's also been far too long since I've seen you." I said, "Well, I've been here." And she said, "Yes, I know. But I didn't know whether you'd want to see me or not." I said, "All you had to do was call to find out."

And so anyway, that's the way it went. And we got back together again. I mean, she was not a person who would push or pressure you, but I knew that this is what she wanted, and if I made a move, she would accept it. So we got back together again, and she moved to New York into an apartment of her own. Since she was working, she later went on to have a larger apartment for her sons to come and stay with her whenever they wanted to, so that was fine. She wasn't too far away from me—it was within walking distance. So it was all right. It went on OK.

Then she became ill, and the doctor said that he thought she needed a hysterectomy. She wanted to go home and have it there because her father was a doctor, and also she wanted to be close to her children. At least her father would suggest the best surgeon he knew of. He had a good reputation as a doctor in the town. So anyway, she went back home and had the hysterectomy, and then she came back and told me she was back with this woman again. And I was really surprised that time, even more so than the first time. I thought, *She's gone through this once. Now she's going back?* And she said, "Well, I needed a place to recuperate, and the woman offered." I guess the woman said, "Come stay with me. You won't have to pay anything." Marion said to me, "You know, I'll be going back and forth to Pennsylvania to see my children, and I'll certainly stop off on the way to see you." So that went on for a while. That was the second time we got back together. But it wasn't satisfactory that time. I didn't know her new address. I never knew where she was. I couldn't, say, call on her if I needed something.

That went on for about a year or more, and then I began to feel like a kept woman. I was available whenever she passed through town, you know. She would call me, and we'd have lunch together, or she'd stop off. And she had a key to the apartment, which she always had from the time I started living there. She'd come in, you know, on Friday night, and spend the weekend. So I couldn't have anyone else there because I wouldn't want someone else there and have her come in. I told her to think of the place as her own. And I don't suppose I should have said that, but I did—and she did. [*Laughs*] You know, she would come in anytime, whether I was expecting her or not. [*Laughs*] And then she'd leave, which was a rather strange arrangement, I felt. I was dissatisfied with it, so finally I broke it off myself. I just said, "Give me back my key; this is the end." [I told her that] I would always like to see her, but she'd have to call me and let me know when she was coming and not expect anything from me except friendship. She accepted this without any comment. And so that was the way it was left.

And then I met a man, and I got married to him. [*Laughs*]

What year was that?

M: That was 1960. I met him in 1959, and I got married in 1960. Then I got divorced in 1961. [*Laughs*]

Did he have any idea?

M: Yeah, he'd known all about me because I'd known him from being in the 12-step program all the while. He used to say to me, "If you ever decide to go straight, let me know." [*Laughs*] He had a great sense of humor, and he was a funny kind of guy. He liked women—he didn't care what persuasion they were. And he didn't try to hassle them to go to bed with him. He never had the idea that "all you need is someone like me," you know, "and then you'll change your mind"—which is what the typical male attitude is. [*Laughs*]

He certainly didn't change yours.

M: No. It didn't last. He was trying to interfere with my friendship with Maggie because he objected to the fact that she came to San Francisco about the same time that I did—we did, my husband and I. It sounds funny to say that. And I never even wrote a letter to Marion telling her. I just moved out. But Jimmy objected every time I wanted to see Maggie, and it got to be a bore. He wasn't bad in bed; I enjoyed going to bed with him, so I guess I'm bisexual. Girls are. But he objected to my seeing anyone he felt I was very emotionally involved with—even a good friend like Maggie. So I thought, *That's it!* I moved out and into this building. Then Jimmy left San Francisco and went back to New York. I guess he decided to file for divorce because there was no point in having legal ties with someone you're not involved with. And he was willing to pay for the divorce, and that was all right with me.

So then I was feeling very much alone here, and I sent Marion a birthday card and told her what I was doing and what had happened. She was glad to hear from me, as always, and she said, "Let's not wait so long between letters." And so I answered that, and a couple times I heard from her.

And then I got a letter from her aunt. It was the Christmas of '61. Her aunt wrote and told me that Marion had had two mastectomies around November, and she'd begun to feel pain all up her back. She had bone cancer. So I thought to myself, *This is it. I know she's going to die.* I just felt it and had to accept that fact. And I decided to go back because—well, I wouldn't say we parted on bad terms, but we never resolved enough. That's the important part of death, you know—you can go easily if you have resolved all of the problems in life, the important problems. And I thought, *Well, I'll go back. I can do that much for her. And perhaps she might even get better.* She hadn't said anything about this being the end, but I felt that it was.

I left at the end of January, and I went back, and I was with her for six weeks before she had to go back to the hospital for the final hospitalization. And we had settled a number of things. And she said that she had broken away from this woman. She said never did she realize that a person could be so overcome by the influence of another person, that this last time Marion had told the woman that she was leaving and for her not to come into her life anymore. I thought it was strange because it happened just about the time I left New York City, and if I had known that, I never would have left. But I didn't know, and she didn't tell me. It was one of those things.

Of course we enjoyed our visit in the beginning. We were very pleased to see each other. And of course the cancer got worse and worse and worse and more difficult to cope with. I could see her getting worse. Her son could see it. He didn't know what to do, and I didn't know what to do with him. All I could do was stay around and be a cheerful helpmate. I cooked for her. I could at least make meals for her that were healthful and tasty.

Then she felt so bad one night that she called the doctor. The pain was too much. She asked him for more medicine. I don't know why he was so worried about her becoming an addict when she had a terminal illness anyway. But he said, "You need to be in the hospital. I can't treat you at home anymore." So she went back to the hospital. I went along and got her settled in as well as possible. She seemed fairly coherent then, and she was taking Demerol. So then I packed my things and went back to New York, and that's the end of the story. I had to find myself a place to live, of course, and as luck would have it, I ran into a person I knew who lived in the building I had lived in, and there was an apartment available. And I was working for *Eros* magazine, in charge of the subscription department.

Then Marion died. It was a fluke that I hadn't heard before because I left my address with them, but I guess it was lost in the shuffle. So I called the doctor's wife, and she told me that Marion had died that Thursday. It was so weird because that Thursday night I had had a dream that I was back with her at her house, her apartment, when she was sick. And I remember when I used to go out, I'd rush back and look in her room to make sure she was still all right. In the dream I did this. I had gone shopping, and I rushed back in the room, and she was standing up and she was all well. There was nothing wrong with her. She looked the way she used to. I apparently must have felt that this had happened, and that she was well in the sense that she was dead and free of all her suffering and whatever was wrong with her, and she was peaceful somewhere. So anyway, that's the end of story.

Did you ever live with anyone again?

M: No, I didn't live with anyone. I had a couple of affairs. I never found anyone I really liked that much. I sort of fell for a girl that I hired. Talk about men hiring girls they're attracted to. I saw this girl come in to apply for a job, and I needed a typist, and so before I even interviewed her I thought to myself, *I'm going to hire her!* [*Laughs*] She was too attractive to let go! I was so glad she could type when I gave her the test. [*Laughs*] There you are! So now I understand men—a little bit, anyway. So then we got to be friends. I was sort of on the rebound, I'm sure, from Marion's death. You know, I was really smitten with her, but it didn't work out. She had a boyfriend somewhere, and she was really not lesbian by nature. I think she did have some leanings to it. She wasn't put off by my interest in her, but she said she'd rather be married to a man. So I let that go.

I stayed in New York for a while longer, and then I came back to San Francisco. That was 1965. I was in New York from 1962 to 1965. Marion died on May 3, 1962, and I was in New York for another three years. *How long were you and Marion together?*

M: Altogether, more than three years. But it seemed that I was always with her spiritually. And in the end we were so close. Some people thought I was silly to go back and see her after all that had happened. They said, "She certainly didn't think too much of you." And I said, "Well, it doesn't matter. I would feel dissatisfied if I didn't resolve this thing." And I think she would have felt very dissatisfied too. I don't think one should let these other types of feelings, like, "You didn't do this, so I can't do that for you," stand in the way. Certain things are much more important than that.

Marion was so creative. Everything she did she brought creativity to, even a relationship, which is what I think made it so great. She was so imaginative about things, about living, and she was so sensitive to people's feelings.

I've heard so many stories. They weren't my story at all. I would call them horror stories—rejection by families, things like that. Not being able to get a job because homosexuality is on your record from school, a woman who realizes that she's a lesbian in school and is found in the dormitory with her girlfriend—these things have happened to people, which I never went through. With me it was all pleasure, practically—except for the back-and-forth with Marion.

Suzanne Judith
Oakland, California

Suzanne Judith occupies the top floor of a funky Victorian-era house in that confusing northeastern section of the city where Emeryville, Berkeley, and Oakland all intersect. The boundaries of the three cities aren't clean—they snake around, changing from block to block, east to west, north to south. The only way to tell where I am from minute to minute is by looking at the street signs: white on blue for Emeryville, black on white for Berkeley, and white on black for Oakland. By the time I find her house and park, I am completely stressed.

But not for long.

Suzanne welcomes me into her home, a tranquil aerie festooned with crystals and chimes and tapestries and swatches of velvety material and cushiony chairs and a sofa that, collectively, make me want to remove my shoes and stay for a good long while.

She makes me a cup of tea and chats comfortably. A light incense hangs in the air. It is no wonder that she is one of the most sought-after Tarot readers and teachers in the Bay Area and the woman whom Tarot expert and author Mary K. Greer has called "a healer, thinker, magician, and mover of Tarot."

"The instant I laid the cards down [for the first time] I said, 'This is for me; this is my language,'" says Suzanne, describing her first experience with the Tarot. "Now I've been doing it for years and years."

Suzanne listens to my questions with the intensity of a therapist: Her attention is keenly focused. Her gestures are animated, and from time to time, she lets out a rib-raising howl of laughter.

"My peasant always comes out," she says amusedly. "It's my family's particular kind of Jewishness, and it's different from the Jewishness of those upper-crust Jewish people like the Swigs, who head up foundations and are millionaires. I come from New York—Ellis Island, the Statue of Liberty, and all that.

"Not only weren't [those greenhorns] middle-class, but before they became working-class, before they started in the sweatshops, they were peasant farmers or peasant villagers, who had tanned leather or made wagon wheels or caught fish. I've been getting in touch with that and kinda having fun with it. I've said to myself, 'OK, you've been trying to suppress this and be a little lady, learned to be more subdued...but it kinda cuts down on my authenticity. I've learned how to be charming about it, making it appealing or attractive, kind of dolling it up a little to make it more presentable and communicate how fine it is. You call someone a peasant—'You peasant!'—it's kind of like an insult, déclassé. I'm reclaiming that. You know, peasants have more fun!"

Interviewed 1987

Avon, the Air Force, and a Feminist Consciousness

You came out with the women's liberation movement.

S: Right. I was 38 at the time. It was like, one day I wasn't [a lesbian], and the next day I was. It was very immediate. And once I was, I knew I had always been. I remembered childhood incidents and girlhood sweethearts, sexual episodes and all these things that I had repressed. Immediately after I had my first experience of making love with another woman—I had this great orgasm and everything—right after that, the next morning, all these memories came flooding back. And I got extremely angry for all the years of repression, and for all the things that had been done to me to thwart that natural direction of growth.

Did you ever read that article on compulsory heterosexuality? Oh, Adrienne Rich! You must! In an issue of *Quest* she wrote this article titled "Compulsory Heterosexuality," and it was very exciting to me. I think I ran into that when I was 45. Someone gave me a Xeroxed copy of it, you know. It was getting passed around. And that was kinda my flashback. When I first came out, I felt that weight of compulsory heterosexuality.

What were the circumstances of your coming out?

S: I was living in Berkeley, and I had two teenage sons, and I had decided that it would be good to live communally. So we had a household of various people. I was the householder, the lease-holder, and had the main responsibility, and I was trying to live this egalitarian lifestyle with all these people. Those were very radical political days. It was 1971, like on the tail end of the Love Generation and the very beginning of the women's liberation movement.

I was already a feminist. I had gone to consciousness-raising meetings. Even how I'd gotten to my first consciousness-raising meeting was a trip. I was working for the Consumers Co-op in Berkeley, in the office doing typesetting with an IBM composer and layout. This office was above the University Avenue store, and I used to go downstairs to the lunch counter and eat my lunch sometimes. And so I was sitting there eating my lunch, and there was this strange sight. It was a woman wearing overalls and boots and no makeup.

She was very beautiful, and it was somehow very surprising to me that she would be beautiful when she wasn't wearing any makeup and wasn't wearing a dress. She had approached these two blue-haired old ladies who were sitting there eating their lunch, and she was telling them about this women's center that had just opened, that it was for women of all ages, and she was inviting them to an open meeting of the women's community that very Friday night. And my ears were going, like, str-e-e-etch. And I thought, *Why isn't she talking to m-e-e-e?* The ladies didn't want to be bothered. They were just eating their lunch, and they were saying, "Yes, dear," you know.

So finally I couldn't stand it anymore. I couldn't keep my eyes on the book I was reading. I was so turned on 'cause I'd felt that I'd been a feminist all my life, and I was just waiting for the women's movement to happen. My consciousness was, like, right there, instantly. It's not like I hadda figure anything out. I was already aware of it and ready to join in right then and there. I had sort of heard of the women's liberation movement, but I thought it was for college girls and happening at the university. I was a working mother, and it didn't seem relevant to me. I thought it was, like, theoretical.

Anyway, I finally approached this woman with the overalls and I said, "I couldn't help overhearing, you know. Does this mean I can come to this meeting too?" She said, "Oh, yeah, sure. By all means, please come." You know, I was in full makeup. I mean, you're looking at someone who used to be an Avon lady. So, I went to the meeting, and I was astonished. There were, like, tons of women there. And after we heard some really rousing talks, they had a panel. One [panelist] talked about how women were demeaned in the media, and another talked about abortion issues, another talked about this and that, and each one had a different presentation. And I was going, "Yeah, yeah, yeah!"

And they had a women's art display going on at the same time, and the piece of art that I remember the best—because it was so astonishing to me—was a garbage can that had the cover off. The cover was sort of hanging off the side, and coming up out of the garbage can was this enormous penis that was red, white, and blue with stars. You know, it was like the flag. And I looked at this thing, and I thought, *Yes, right. That's the problem!* I was, like, very excited.

At that point I had broken up with my—I wouldn't have called him a boyfriend, I'd say my old man—and I'd made up my mind that I was through with them forever. That was the last straw. There wasn't anything that they could do for me that I couldn't do for myself. I thought, *I have my friends, I have my kids,* and who needed them? You know, the sex was good, but you always had all these other trips you had to deal with because of them, and I wasn't getting my needs met, and I didn't want to be in those relationships. Every relationship with a man that I ever had had certain features that were similar that I really didn't like.

So I was being a celibate and was being a militant political activist. I was in the lunatic fringe. I was doing actions. I was putting my anger at the target. There was this whole thing about realizing how angry I was about female oppression and getting directly involved in doing things that would get that anger out at the target and make a difference and cause a revolution. The idea was to turn over as little money in the economy as possible, and the whole economy would crash. And if enough people would do that, we were sure it was really going to happen. A lot of us took poverty baths. There were free boxes, and people recycled things and used stuff they would have thrown out and salvaged. And we had all sorts of bartering going on. There were food buying co-operatives—we'd meet in people's living rooms and weigh up all the stuff. And people were tearing down fences between yards and making big gardens in the middle of blocks. We were doing a lot of alternative things. Everybody was going to meetings; everybody was very political. Oh, it was a very yeasty atmosphere, you know.

It was the beginnings of women's culture, the very, very beginning. There was this newspaper, *It Ain't Me Babe*, and there were women's poetry readings at the Unitarian Church. There were women there playing guitar and singing songs that they had made up. It was just beginning to happen.

At this point, I left the Co-op and got my own IBM composer. The name of my little typesetting and layout business was called Amazon Graphics. This was way before lesbians adopted the name Amazon. I took the name Amazon because it conjured the image of a big woman, and I was fat. And I had started wearing overalls and boots too, and Hawaiian shirts and all kinds of outlandish outfits. That way when people arrived at my shop, it said "Amazon," and here I was. I might not have been tall, but it explained something about my size and perhaps my stance. Because once I became a feminist, I no longer would take any crap off of anybody. I was totally into holding my own and being cooperative but not accommodating. My personality changed a lot, and it was wonderful. I used to be something of a doormat. I know it doesn't seem possible now, but it was really true. It was the whole Avon lady, Air Force–wife thing, but that was too long ago.

So anyway, I met this woman who read poetry. I was at the Co-op, shopping for the commune. There were a lot of us, and I always ended up with three baskets of groceries for the week. I didn't know how to drive in those years—I didn't learn to drive until I was 42—so I always hadda call a taxi to get home, even though it was only, maybe, five or six blocks. And I always used to call Taxi Unlimited. It was Berkeley's free taxi, you know, with the wildly-painted cabs and the trippy guys smoking joints. I was really into that. I couldn't be a full hippie because I was a working mother, but that was my direction.

So anyway, I spied this woman poet in the Co-op, and I knew her name was Amy. I knew her, so I thought, *Maybe she'll give me a ride home with my groceries.* So, she gives me a ride home, and I said, "Well, c'mon in. Would you like a cup of tea?" "Sure," you know. So we ended up with coffee around the kitchen table, and she was kind of mind-boggled. I had this one son who was kind of a flaming faggot with long Cinderella locks, and my other son was a Jimi Hendrix rock 'n' roll-nik. And so there were all these strange people at the kitchen table, including a gay guy in nun drag and some others. People were wearing costumes a lot in Berkeley those days. Everybody would dress very outlandishly just to go anywhere. That was part of the style. So there were very interesting, atypical conversations going on, and she was quite apparently taken by the scene.

So, she took to hanging out at our kitchen table a lot, and she became a really good friend of mine. And somewhere along the line she mentioned that she was a lesbian, and I said, "Well, hey, different strokes for different folks! That's cool. You know, I'm a feminist—I love all women." [*Laughs*]. You know, before the women's movement I never used to hug or kiss women. I thought it was so weird with all that mushy stuff, you know, coming together, kissing a woman. But once the women's movement started happening, you were supposed to greet your sisters warmly and, you know, hug them. Sort of like Frenchmen kissing each other on the cheek or even on the lips. They were sisters, right? And I never had a sister, so I was very thrilled 'cause suddenly I had all these sisters, and I could kiss them hello and good-bye and hug them, and it was really wonderful.

And that was one of the wonderful things about this new friendship. You know, we used to stay up and gab for hours, and it was great. And I got interested in her poetry, and I used to go to her readings.

As it was getting closer to, like, blast-off time, I remember her saying something about lesbians this and that. And I said, "Yes! And *we* this and that." And I thought, *Now, why'd I say* we*? I'm not a lesbian. Oh, well, it doesn't matter—I'm a sister!* And I just went on. But she heard that with a capital *W-E,* you can bet! [*Laughs*]

In the meantime, other friends of mine were coming out left and right. All these feminists were turning to each other for love, and I'd say, "Congratulations, you have my blessing," and, "Love is wonderful, whatever form it takes."

And then came this fateful time when Amy wanted to come over to visit, and I wanted her to come over, but her car was broken down. So I got one of the guys in the commune to go over and pick her up for me. And she came over, and we drank coffee, and we talked and talked and talked. And pretty soon it was 1 or 2 o'clock in the morning, and she didn't have the money for a taxi, and it was too late for the bus, and all the guys in the commune had gone to sleep. And I said, "Hey, you can spend the night. My son"—the gay one—"is away for the weekend, and he's got a nice bedroom and a really big bed up there. C'mon, I'll show you where it is."

We got to the foot of the stairs, and I got this funny feeling like, *Uh-oh, I better not go upstairs. I don't have to go all the way. I'll just tell her which door it is.* Somehow the atmosphere was very charged. I wasn't sure why, you know. So I said, "Yeah, you just go right to the end of the hall; you can't miss it. It's the door immediately at the end of the hall." She says, "OK, great. Thanks a lot." And then it was like, we usually hug and kiss good-bye when she's gonna leave or walk out the door. And then I thought, *OK, I guess we could give each other a kiss good night instead of good-bye, even though she's just going upstairs. There's no reason we shouldn't.* [*Laughs*]

So we started hugging each other. And all of a sudden, I really didn't want her to let go, and she wasn't letting go, and we just stood there holding each other for what seemed a long time. And I thought, *What's going to happen now?* And so we finally ended up going upstairs together, and that was that. I went to bed that night with her, and it was wonderful! And then the next morning, all these memories came flooding in.

What did you remember?

S: I started out remembering stuff from when I was five years old—and I still have this vision so strongly. I was sitting on the front stoop of this house in Brooklyn. It was my friend's house, and it had these stone lions on either side of the steps. And we were talking about masturbating. And I was saying, "Yeah, it feels really good on that cushiony little thing." I remember I said that. And she said, "Yeah." And we both agreed that it was the *haps*, you know. She was my best friend then, when I was a very little girl, and I had that same friend from when I was five to when I was a young wife. I know we used to fool around with each other, and I know she was the first love of little girlfriends.

I always had these special best friends, and they were always really passionate, even though I don't actually remember doing anything with them. But then I remembered in grade school how I actually contrived, unconsciously, to touch this other girl's breasts. We were all clustered around an upright piano, and we were singing. She was standing next to me, and I saw that if I sort of put my elbow on the top of the piano, and it sort of slipped down a little bit, I could kind of nudge her breasts with my arm.

I thought she wouldn't notice! [*Laughs*] She noticed! She got really uptight and made a big ruckus in school. OK, and then that died down and went away.

And then we moved from Brooklyn into the suburbs, and I got this new best friend, who was a year younger than me, who wasn't in my class. Her name was Barbara, and we became inseparable. My folks gave me a new bicycle, and I learned to ride it, and Barbara and I went everywhere on our bikes. And she turned me on to horseback riding. There was a stable not too far from where we lived, and we would work. We shoveled horse manure. As many hours as we would shovel manure, we could then trade for taking out any horse that was available for that many hours. First we had to learn riding and practice in the ring, and so we traded for that. Eventually we got to where we could take the horses out, and we could go anywhere we wanted, and we knew where all the trails were, and we'd go riding together.

How old were you?

S: She was 12, and I was 13. And we'd take our bikes during those golden summers, and we'd go to the beach and go swimming. And we'd take our bikes out to the state park where there was a carousel, and we'd catch the brass ring. We'd sing all these songs. We both liked to sing, and we'd harmonize. We were also both really interested in philosophy and metaphysics, except we didn't call it metaphysics. We used to talk about the universe and existence. We said, "You know, if grown-ups ever knew what we were talking about, they wouldn't believe it! They think we're just kids, but we know what's happening."

We liked to go to the Museum of Modern Art and look at Picasso. We liked jazz. We liked Charlie Parker, and we thought that all those kids who liked Bing Crosby and Frank Sinatra were really squares, and we were really hip. It was hard to be allowed to go to the city ourselves, but if we were really good, we could talk our folks into it, knowing that as soon as we got a few blocks away from the house, we'd put on lipstick, and we'd go to Greenwich Village. If we were supposed to go see a certain movie, we'd have to go see that movie so we could come back and tell them about it. We were pretty far-out, avant-garde little girls, and we had lots of good times.

When we were in school we had different classes, but we would walk home from school together, and then I'd have to go my way, and she would have to go hers. And then, as soon as we'd get home, we'd call each other up and talk for hours. We'd go to the soda fountain together, and we'd go shopping together. We'd even go shoplifting together. [*Laughs*]

In the meantime, in school there'd be these parties. It wasn't happening in her class yet because she was only 12. But in my class we played spin the bottle and post office, and we'd have these contests for the best kisser and whether you could do this back-bend kiss like in the Tabu perfume ads. You know, it was very Hollywood-oriented and very Errol Flynn, and the boys would tango or something and get you in this back bend, leaning you over and holding you back while they kissed you as though you fainted or swooned from the kiss. The more dramatic and sizzling you could make the kiss, the more Hollywood-like, and also how long you held the kiss would determine who won. And there'd be these little prizes, and the one who was giving the party would get little things from Woolworths. [*Laughs*]

So, I was going to some of these parties, and I thought, *Gee, pretty soon Barbara's class is going to be having these kissing games, and wouldn't it be nice if she could win some of the prizes because she already knew how? And I could teach her!* [*Laughs*] So I introduced the idea of [kissing] practice. She was kind of interested in the boys too but not too confident of her ability. I mean, she knew that you weren't supposed to let them touch you "down there" or up here [*motions to her breasts*]. We both knew the facts of life and how you get a baby and all that, but neither one of us was terribly confident of our skills at necking. We knew that the boys were going to try and feel us up and we weren't supposed to let them, but I wondered what it would feel like when they did. If we tried it out on each other, then we'd know what it was going to feel like when they did it to us. And we should practice, so we'd know whether or not we really wanted to say no or not.

So we began practicing, and that became a part of what we did, besides everything else. We had horseback riding, picnicking, and also *practice*. We also practiced dance steps and singing, so this became another wonderful thing that we did, and it seemed appropriate and natural somehow.

Barbara had this family of five brothers and sisters, among whom were these two totally gorgeous older sisters who both played the violin in the symphony orchestra. Each was more beautiful than the next, and they had all these boyfriends. One of them was 19, and the other was 21 or something like that. And so, they were going out on a double date to the beach, and their dates were coming to get them in a station wagon, and they invited us to come along. We were thrilled! We figured out that the reason they invited us was to keep the boys from getting too fresh, so the little sister and her friend were coming along. People would lay on the beach and start embracing, and you'd want to keep control. We were both thrilled because we adored these two sisters, and letting us come on a grown-up date—wowie-zowie.

They put us in the tailgate section, and that put us kind of lying down. They had two in the front, two in the middle, and we were in the back. So, we were lying there, and it was a real beautiful day, and the sky was flashing past, and we were close, and we just naturally fell into practicing. It just sort of happened. All of a sudden one of the sisters happened to look back, and she screamed, "What are you doing!" We said, "We're practicing." We figured she had a boyfriend, and she'd understand that we were practicing to do what they did, and there was nothing wrong with it.

It made perfect sense to you.

S: Yeah! And she said, "Practicing what?" And I said, "Practicing for the kissing games." And she said—and I'll never forget this—"Well, kissing is one thing, but trading spit is something else!" And I thought, *She's lying.* I had seen these movies—those big close-ups where two faces came together, the lips opening. I had seen these things with my own eyes. I knew she had been to the movies as much as me, and I knew that when she kissed her boyfriend it wasn't like she was kissing Aunt Etta. I knew she opened her mouth with her boyfriend. And I thought, *She's just acting like a grown-up!* We thought that they were our buddies and sisters. She said, "Stop doing that immediately!" And we said, "OK," and we started singing.

It was not a big thing. I mean, it was, and it wasn't. 'Cause what happened then was, we all had a wonderful day at the beach. It was terrific. You know, everything was copacetic. And then we went home. She dropped me off, and later that evening I got a phone call from Barbara, and she said, "I can't see you anymore." She said she couldn't talk to me anymore. But we were in the same school, and I'd see her in the hall, and she'd look right through me. And I said, "Why?" And she said, "I can't explain it." And I said, "But what did I do? How come?" And she said, "Well, my parents think you're too fast." I said, "Too fast?" I didn't know what she was talking about. I said, "What do you mean 'too fast'?" And she said, "Well, they think you're too advanced for me." And she said, "Look, I can't talk about it. We just have to stop being friends." And I said, "What if I saved your life?" And she said, "It wouldn't make any difference."

I was totally devastated, just devastated.

So, like I say, the morning after I came out, after I'd had that lovemaking experience, it all came back—the stone lions, the piano nudging. Those are the main ones, but since then I've had memories of other women that I've adored, other best friends, who you weren't openly sexual with, but there was open, declared love.

Did you ever hear the word "lesbian"?

S: By the time I got to be a late teenager I had heard the word, and I didn't think it was me at all because how I thought they were was that they all wore T-shirts and had bulging muscles with tattoos and wore leather jackets. They wore crew cuts, and they were more rough and tough than guys. And they did unspeakable things to you—things that were so terrible that I couldn't even say what they were because you wouldn't want to know. It was too awful.

Now that I look back, the association was with S/M, and I still don't like S/M. And they all smoked cigarettes, and they were tough like truck drivers. [*Laughs*] And you hardly ever saw one, but if you saw a woman who looked like that, then she was one, and you should avoid her at all costs. I mean, I would still avoid a woman who looked like that. I had no idea that the word lesbian referred to the entire gamut of women.

That began to change when I saw my friends coming out. And I remember one time when I was with my old man—well, I had various ones, but this particular one, I was with him for about four years—and we were over in Sausalito. I had friends in a houseboat community, which at the time was not this slick, commercial thing, but it was hippies living the hippie life on trippy boats, which were patched together and fixed up and psychedelic. It was quite an interesting little community out there.

My old man was a plumber, and I was working civil service, and on weekends we used to go out to Sausalito and be hippies and get someone to look after the kids. And this one particular time, we didn't have someone's phone number, and we pulled up to this bar because he wanted me to go in and use the phone book and make the call. So he wanted to wait in the car while I did that. OK, so I go in there, and it's a *women's* bar. I think it doesn't exist anymore because I don't know of any women's bar in Sausalito. But I was totally astonished. I had never been in such a place before.

How did the women look?

S: Oh, they didn't look like those truck drivers! There were some who looked a little bit like that, but most of them didn't. And they were all there, and there was a woman bartender, and there were no men. That's how I knew it was a women's bar—there were no men. And I was, like, *What is this?* It was like I was on Mars or something. I thought, *I better get out of here pretty quick; this is a weird place. I don't belong here.* But then I thought, *I've been in a bar before. I'm bold, and I'm bad, and I can hold my own in this situation.*

So, I got change from the bartender, and I hadda walk to the back where the phone was, and it was crowded. And the thing I noticed that was so unusual was that usually if a woman is going someplace, people will automatically move a few inches out of the way so that she can pass without making bodily contact—just, like, a little politeness among straight people that they kind of make way for you so you don't have to brush against them. Well, I had to get to the phone booth, and as I say, it was quite crowded, and these women didn't move out of the way in that kind of automatic don't-touch-me way. There was a little yielding so that I could get by, but there was unavoidable body contact as I made my way through. They brushed up against me, and I was kind of uptight about it.

I made my phone call, and I got out of there. You know, I just kinda brushed back out the door. Phew! And I got back in the car, and I said, "Wow, Eddie, that was a real weird bar!" And he said, "What do you mean?" "Well, it was all women in there!" And he said, "Oh, *bulldaggers*." That was a new word. There wasn't anybody I had seen in there that went with that word, bull and dagger. You know, it sounded kinda like bulldog, and there was nobody like that either. And I said, "Oh, is that what you call them?" And he said, "Yeah, and if anyone gave you any shit, you shoulda called me." "Oh, no, no. It was OK, nobody bothered me."

But that experience—it was such a small experience. I mean, in four years with this man you would think that I would have forgotten it. There were millions of things that happened with him that I forgot, but that one stood out and is indelible in my memory and also came back to me that next morning after I had been with Amy. And I thought about it and said, "Yes, it was kinda weird, but I liked that they didn't move out of the way." A part of me may have been scared, but essentially, I kind of liked it. So that once [I made love with a woman] I knew that I had been a lesbian from the beginning of whenever.

See, I didn't call it "lesbianism," but my mother knew that my friend Barbara had stopped playing with me and that I was really brokenhearted. And I think that she maybe called Barbara's parents to find out why. But this was never spoken of. And I think that she knew I was really grieving, and she tried to do things to get my mind off it. It was a totally taboo subject in our household, and I sorta knew that.

Years later I did eventually come out to my mother. She's sort of the don't-want-to-know type. I remember telling her my son Seth was gay. I had gone back to New York for a visit. We were sitting in this diner having coffee, and she told me that the Danish pastry at the diner was very good. They had a good variety, different kinds. OK, so we're sitting there, and we were drinking coffee and trying to decide what pastry to have, and she says, "So, is Seth dating yet?" He was 17 or so. And I said "dating?"—thinking that he was this queen and "dating" wasn't exactly what he called it. And she said, "Well, the only reason that I ask is that he is 17, and usually around that age they get interested in the opposite sex." And I said, "Oh, well, in Seth's case that's not likely to happen because he's mostly focused on members of his own sex."

And then mom said, "Would you like a Danish? Prune?" And I said, "No, cheese."

So, when it came to telling her about myself, I thought, *She's not really gonna want to hear this.* But I was so in love with this woman. I was so happy, and I was talking to my mother on the phone, and she said, "So, how are things going?" And I said, "Well, I'm really at a very happy time of my life." And she said, "Oh, yeah?" And I said, "Yeah, I'm in love." And she said, "Well, who is it?" And I said, "I'm in love with this woman!" And she said, "What about Gene?" That was my last boyfriend. And I said, "Oh, I still love him, but I'm not with him." And that was true, I mean, I never stopped loving him; I just wasn't that interested in him anymore. Well, she just changed the subject the way she did with the Danish. It was, like, don't look at it, and it will go away.

Then every now and then, something would come up, and I wasn't into being in the closet. I really wanted to be out to everyone. I never wanted to be in the closet. I'd felt I'd already spent enough years in the unconscious closet; I was in the closet to myself. I didn't even know about myself. I was in the closet of the closet. No way! Once I came out, and all those memories came flooding back, I thought, *There is no way that I'd ever put my personality in a girdle like that again and repress my own natural impulses and inclinations.* So I didn't really care what her reaction was. I knew she wasn't going to like it because she was very into being conventional, and I have always been the reverse—very unconventional.

Also, the climate of the times was like, come out! It was a political act, and I was very much riding on that wave. But even though times have changed a lot, I'm still into being out, pretty much. There have been times when I thought, *Well, I'm not going to wear a warm, fuzzy dyke button, but if anyone asks me I'll be open about it, but I don't have to say* "I am a lesbian!" *Are they going around saying* "I am straight!" *They are making assumptions about me, which is very annoying.*

But what I'm noticing is that because I'm older, people tend to neuter me anyway. Because I'm older and because I'm fat—both of those things combined—younger straight people—that is, straight people in their 20s, 30s, and 40s—tend to do this. Since they suppose that all women are straight anyway, and since they suppose all middle-age women are over-the-hill anyway, they just conveniently neuter me. So all I have to do is not mention my sexuality or my social preferences, and they'll just assume, and I can be a person and not have to be tilting at windmills all the time.

Sometimes I think that everyone is born bisexual and that the reason that some of us are lesbians—and I include myself in this—is that the patriarchy is so oppressive that it's really impossible to relate to a man and have it be an equitable relationship. But other times I don't think that at all. Other times I think that some women are just born lesbians. They just have those inclinations. For instance, take a look at Judy Grahn—you just cannot imagine that she ever seriously got into going to the prom and having a strapless evening gown. Whereas me—yeah, I once did go to a prom and had a strapless evening gown. I was really into looking good and having my nail polish and going to the beauty parlor and that kind of stuff. You know, I really got into that for a while. And I was very focused on having a boyfriend and having dates and all of that. In fact, there was a period in my life when I didn't like girls. But then again, when I was 14 I borrowed my father's trousers and my father's flannel shirt to go horseback riding, and I liked that! And then I got very interested in my father's neckties. I got him to show me how you tie these different necktie knots, and I asked him if I could wear one of his neckties with one of my blouses to school. And he let me do that. And I started wearing different neckties everyday to school, and that was part of my way of being unconventional. See, there were all these little hints.

So, in terms of being born that way, what I really think now is that some women are born that way for reasons that we don't know and that other women figure it out as they go. And that other women fall into it accidentally and discover they love it. And that some women never do get around to it. Maybe most women. But I do think that it's a natural impulse because every little girl starts in by falling in love with her mother or a mothering figure. I think that at some point you do fall in love with Daddy, but that's secondary. Just like that song that Alix Dobkin used to sing, "Everyone Woman Can Be a Lesbian"—every woman has loved a woman more than anything or anyone else. I think that every woman has it in her and that it's natural.

Trudy Genovese
Somewhere in New England

Trudy Genovese lives in a rustic New England cottage, sagging for want of a foundation, ringed by sugar maples, aspen, and birch, wild berries, a red-cherry tree, and a thatch of milkweed that she planted especially for the Monarch butterflies who favor its taste.

"That's my contribution to Monarchville," she says, running her hands through her short white hair.

Her yard is a haven for red foxes, deer, horned owls, and raccoons, and she tells me of a neighbor who once came home to find a bear amidst the emptied contents of his refrigerator.

"Poor things," she says, shaking her head in concern. "The bears are more active this year because they're hungry. It has been such a dry season, and all the berries just shriveled and dropped to the ground."

Trudy, 61, wears a sailor's denim work shirt, denim painter's pants, and suede slippers. Although she has agreed to talk with me, she seems wary. Her blue eyes turn from suspicion to amusement as I pass Litmus tests and interrogation, which culminate in the question: "So, are you gay?"

"Yes," I say, surprised, pointing to my Joan of Arc hair and engineer boots.

"That doesn't mean anything," says Trudy, unmoved. "Straight girls shave their heads and wear combat boots today. Clothing doesn't mean a thing!" She is missing front teeth, but even so, she is very handsome.

"You've been at this long enough to know that 99% of us don't want

to talk; it's a matter of survival. I don't think that you can understand the fear," she adds.

Inside we sit at a battered kitchen table with a red Formica top. She serves us steaming mugs of coffee, strong and black. My student assistant, Inna, asks for milk and sugar, which Judy ribs her for.

"You?" she says to me.

"Black!"

"Now you're talking!" she says, and pours herself the same from a 1960s-vintage stainless steel electric coffeepot, which in this age of coffeemakers is hardly ever seen anymore.

Trudy is a retired computer programmer and self-described pack-rat, and her home fairly bursts with old computers and keyboards, books, paper, and boxes. Her girlfriend, she says, is in the middle of re-arranging things.

"So she gives the place a makeover," she shrugs. "What's a little manipulation when you're having so much fun?"

Interviewed September 1996

Most Butches
Are Excellent Cooks

T: You have heard of Provincetown?

Of course! I've been there.

T: Provincetown, in the good old days, was our Mecca. That's where all of us went in the summer.

All of the women from New England?

T: All of the women from New England, New Jersey, Eastern

Seaboard, even Canada. Tremendously large Canadian contingent, male and female, we're talkin'—not just women. P-town has never been [only] women; it's been everybody. This is back when we were all in this together, which was beautiful, and in my life we still are all in this together, which upsets the separatists no end. I'm sorry, sweetie, but you know, we *are* all in this together.

In Provincetown we could be ourselves. There was the Ace of Spades; it was my favorite place of all the places in P-town because it was down an alley, and it was dark. Now people say, "Why do you want to go down an alley in the dark?" You felt safe, that's why.

In New York in the '40s and the '50s, you had to know where places were. Usually they were downstairs. Usually they were Mafia-protected. You would go into a place—if you had never been there before, and you were not with someone who was well-known—and the room that had been full of sound before you got there became absolutely silent. And everybody would be staring at you. It was a weird, weird feeling.

Were the patrons trying to assess whether you were undercover cops?

T: Undercover or God knows what. [*Laughs*] And another unique aspect of New York City was that there were no gay bars—they were all cafés, which meant that you were obliged to order a hamburger, whether you wanted one or not.

So you couldn't go in and have just a beer?

T: You could not. Eventually you could, but initially, because they could not operate as bars, only as cafés, you had to go in and eat the greasy stuff while you were sized up. Now, as time progressed, people were drinking, and it was all right, it was cool. But in the original old days, these were dark holes. You should read *Zami*. Audre Lorde mentions this place and the rest of the places that we actually went.

What were the chain boys?

T: Teenagers with tire chains. And they'd come out and crouch down and rattle them along the sidewalk.

If they saw you?

T: If they saw you. And they hung around the places where they *would* see you. This was sport to these young punks. The closest call I ever had with these boys was one night when I was running around with this girl, Big Jere. I mean, this girl was about 6 foot tall and weighed about 250 pounds. This was a large and well-built Amazon-type woman. [*Laughs*] And this one dear little boy [screamed], "C'mon, you motherfucker!" And she stopped, and she looked down, and she said, "Oh, I'm sorry; I didn't know that was your mother." [*Laughs*] And the other kid, you know—scoff, scoff.

Was she a "passing" woman, Big Jere?

T: Well, I don't know what passing means in the context of today. A passing woman in those days was a woman who was passing for a male. Very few of us were. I only knew one who was—Redsie. Redsie was sort of married to Polly for 23 years before they broke up. Redsie, during the war, was a photographer. She couldn't be a photographer before or after the war because she was only a woman, but during the war she was a photographer. After the war they said, "Well, you can't be a photographer anymore because the men are back." She said, "The hell I can't," and she started passing. And with a name like "Red" rather than "Agnes," she got away with it. And this is another golden attribute of the era—she and her lover, Polly, lived in the suburbs. This is before washers and dryers, now; only the rich had those. So Redsie wore men's shorts. And the world today says that is disgusting when a woman goes so far as to emulate a man by wearing men's shorts! We're not talking emulation. She put a zipper in hers, and she carried her lighter and cigarettes. It was the funniest damn thing. She'd unzip her pants, reach in and pull them out. I mean, that was a hoot and a half right there! But the main thing is, you do the laundry, you put it out on the line. Do you want 27 little ladies' flimsies, or do you want men's shorts and women's panties? It just stood to reason. So Redsie wore men's shorts. I mean, we held these truths to be self-evident.

You have said that when you were younger, you would walk down the streets and pass as a teenage boy. When did you first start doing that?

T: When I was 15. It was a safety thing. I thought I was the only one in the world. And then I found out I was not the only one in the world. I found that out sort of circuitously. I read in the *Herald Tribune,* "Homosexuals Arrested in Street Sweep." And I figured that's what I was. I was thrown out of the library, in the research room, trying to find out what in the hell I was. And everything that I had found said that men were homosexuals, women weren't. There was no mention of gay women. I hadn't even heard of Stephen [the character Stephen Gordon] in *The Well of Loneliness,* and there was no literature until the early '50s, so when I was a teenager, you know, I was just *nada.* [*Laughs*]

Then I got involved with a very nice older woman. I was 14, and she was 17. I was really passing through a hell of a "stage" because she was not the first. But this one—her mother found out, and I was the bad guy. And this, I suppose, is a typical mother thing—she told all of the other mothers in the neighborhood, "We've got a queer on the loose; keep your daughters on a short chain." Which netted my being shunned by just about everybody in the neighborhood. Now where the hell am I gonna go? So I thought, *I'll go to New York and see what's over there.*

So I hopped on the bus, and I went to New York, and I lived in the Village because that's where all the queers were. And I found a copy of *One,* the newsletter of the Mattachine Society, and in the copy of *One* there was a column about women. Oh, God help us! I was home! So I proceeded from there. That was the beginning of my real life, which led to being picked up in street sweeps.

Tell me about street sweeps.

T: Street sweeps. If you were walking down the street or approaching in or out of a bar, and there was a convention in town—before [Mayor] Lindsay, before Kennedy—you were considered a public nuisance, and you were picked up and taken downtown. And this is where I got into a hassle with [historian] Joan Nestle because she called the Women's House of Detention on Greenwich Street in the Village the "House of D." We didn't call it that. We called it the "country club." You know, "Where were you last Saturday night?" "Oh, I was at the country club." A very casual, offhand thing.

And that was a trip and a half. You'd be loaded into the paddy wagon—just because you were there, mind you. I mean, if the kids on the street didn't get you, the cops would half the time. And you were taken to this triangular building, downstairs to the cages—literal cages—taken in front of the desk sergeant, and the desk sergeant would say, "Guilty or not guilty?" It was not until a few years ago that it occurred to me that nobody ever said *what* I was guilty or not guilty of. But we all felt so guilty, and the rule was that if you said "guilty," you could pay $5 and leave.

And if you said "not guilty"?

T: If you said "not guilty," or you didn't say anything, then you went back down to the cage for the night, which was kind of exciting to a point—but the point was soon reached. But $5 in those days was a damn lot of money. But still and all, it was worth it because you had been with your own kind.

And when the cops would go down the street, sweeping, did they look for women in men's clothing, men in women's clothing?

T: Anybody who looked different. Now, I always heard the thing that you had to have three articles of women's clothing. I always heard it. And I suppose I always did it, but I never in my life had anybody check to see if I was wearing any articles of women's clothing.

Well, in San Francisco that is still a law that is on the books. Not observed, naturally, or we'd all be busted.

T: You see, in New York when I was just coming out—coming out in the context of admitting to myself, finding who I was and where I belonged—I would go through a total transition uptown at the old bus station. I would go in as a girl person, and I would leave the bus station as a boy person.

You changed in the bathroom?

T: No, I changed in the alley. How could you change in the bathroom? My God, you'd be crucified.

Did you carry your clothes around in a little knapsack?

T: In a purse. [*Laughs*] In my purse, which I then left in a dime slot in the old bus station. This is before Port Authority. This is when the bus station was a block between 42nd and 43rd, or it might have been 41st and 42nd, but you pulled in. It was just beyond Broadway. Oh, God! Dirty, smelly, what have you.

So, you'd walk in as a woman...

T: I'd walk in as a woman, and walk out as a boy.

That must have been a very big purse.

T: No, it didn't have to be. Not really. Because in those days we had the full skirts—well, you wouldn't know. Hell, you're just a kid yourself! I could wear slacks under my skirt because it was the day of poodle skirts and the broomstick skirts and things like that. So you could wear slacks underneath them. All you needed was a credible shirt and a cap.

And you would roll up trousers underneath the poodle skirt?

T: Oh, absolutely, absolutely. So there was no problem there.

And what about shoes?

T: Shoes were shoes. Nobody paid that much attention. I mean, this is the day of saddle oxfords, for God's sake. Everybody wore saddle oxfords or penny loafers or such like that. No big deal about that. This is the late '40s, before work boots and brogans. Nobody would be seen in New York City in work boots. So that was not a problem.

The big problem was the hair. And I had a pageboy. And I had stale beer. Other people used other things, but that was all I knew about—stale beer. Just slick it back. A very effective DA. And that was that. Of course, the damn stuff was so fine anyway that my pageboy always went limp and just hung kind of stupid-like, but with the beer you could just kind of sweep your hair back. And it got me by. Believe me, it got me by. Because a DA, essentially, is long hair. It's what the greasers had—DAs. What the hell, I'm a blond greaser! What can I tell you? Oh, glory days.

And so you'd walk out of the alley transformed.

T: I'd take the subway down to 23rd and Houston or whichever subway I took. And this was sort of a way of life until we got John Lindsay and John Kennedy. And these two boys, between them, decided sort of unilaterally, categorically, that gays, queers, were not bad for business; they were *good* for business. So Lindsay said, "Don't pick 'em up anymore." The cops didn't obey him half the time, but that's what Lindsay said. Because [gay men and lesbians] were an attraction; people came down to see them. And Kennedy did a totally devastating thing—he changed our camping areas and a lot of our "private" beaches on the Cape to "public" and invited the straights in to gawk at the queers in P-town. I've never forgiven him for that. That was the end of the Ace of Spades, which was my favorite of all the dark bars. Joan Nestle writes about the Sea Colony. The Sea Colony was not from the '40s and '50s. The Sea Colony was from later. The Sea Colony was bright, brightly lighted. Panes of glass on the front window. You know? I mean, what are you telling me? It's not downstairs. It's not in the dark. You could see people when you walked in. People are dancing. This is patronizing. I did not like the Sea Colony. I did not feel comfortable in the Sea Colony. But that's what we had after things opened up, and we were allowed to walk down the street. It really didn't make that much difference on the streets. There were still guys with chains. There were still cops hassling you. If they couldn't take us to the cages, they would still make sure that you were damned uncomfortable.

But of course, three or four decades later everything is wide open in P-town.

T: Well, even in New York in the '60s we had friends on the vice squad who would tell us which bars were going to be raided, so we just didn't go to them. Matter of fact, one gay guy vice cop was going with a Greek Orthodox priest, who regularly married us to whoever we happened to be with at that point in time, on the roof of a tenement on East 80-something. I forget what the street was.

What was that like being in a raid?

T: Absolutely terrifying. The lights would flash, and you knew that trouble was coming. You'd go under the table. That was your first option—you weren't safe there—or out the door. Half the time you didn't know where the door was, unless you'd been frequenting that bar a long, long time. You know, the regulars did, but the rest of us didn't. But it was truly incredible—they never asked your name. They never asked anything. They never told you what you were accused of. It was just, get them off the streets and deprive the bar of business. That, essentially, to my mind, was what it was all about.

Now, the bars could be raided for any number of reasons—either they hadn't paid up, or someone was mad at them. The Mafia owned the place, traditionally. I mean, everybody knew it, but I can't prove it. [*Laughs*] And the cops were in on the take. If the cops didn't get enough from the bar or whoever the hell they were getting it from, they would raid the place. It was a very exciting way to live. Everybody was in somebody else's pocket.

Were you ever beaten up in jail?

T: Oh, yeah. Surprise—by a woman. I was raped by a woman in jail. I did not appreciate that. It didn't cure me.

That seems more male behavior. But a woman actually attacked you?

T: It was a power thing. I've never known why. Never figured it out. A matron—I mouthed off to her.

Did you think she was gay?

T: Didn't have the vaguest. I was terrified.

Was she large?

T: In my eyes, yes. [*Laughs*] I have no idea. What's to compare? She was the power; I was the glory.

And did she also beat you up?

T: Well, I didn't exactly submit. There is a certain element of swinging and flailing in a situation, an arrest situation—"move along, hands on your head, spit nickels, bend over," and all that sort of stuff. It's not a gentle procedure. They didn't have to be gentle because we were queer. [*Laughs*] Or my favorite thing—for some strange reason there was a tendency for people to say we were "*pre*verts," and that always tickled the hell out of me. I have no idea why they confused *per*vert with *pre*vert, but they did. I was called a prevert a damn lot more than I was called a pervert. That is certainly funny.

Do you think it was harder on lesbians or gay men in jail?

T: In jail? I don't know. I was never a gay man in jail. The House of D was strictly women. The men had their own. But we were the ones that they were definitely picking on at that point in time.

You see, after the war we were supposed to be there for men. And any indication in a convention city that a woman was out on the street not as a streetwalker and not for a man—we were fair game. You could be picked up. Because the prevailing view was, all you need is a good man, and you're cured. So it was a challenge match. If the cops could pick up a couple of queer women or one queer woman, there was no protection at all for her. Which explains why numbers of us made a fairly adequate living on the street. You see, if you felt nothing, it was very profitable. I would say that better than 50% of the girls that worked the streets, that I knew, were queer, were gay. But the men—they paid. We all had our women, and that was where the emotions were. But on the street, no. No reaction, no feeling. We just closed off. It was business as usual, what can I tell you?

Did you walk the streets?

T: Oh, yeah. What else was I going to do? I also went to night school. God, what a life. And I lived, and that is the most astonishing thing.

Let me go back to the library, when you were a teenager and were kicked out for trying to look up homosexual material in the adult research room.

T: I was 13 or 14 years old.

And you didn't find anything that described lesbians or female homosexuals.

T: I didn't know the word "lesbian." How would I find it?

What did you think of yourself?

T: I thought I was different. I knew I was different; I did not know *how* I was different. You know, I didn't know if I was the only one in the world who was different. But I sure as hell knew I was different. And all the other girls would express interest in boys. No, no—I didn't feel that way. It's a lonely feeling, a feeling of isolation. So I figured, we're talking a psychological problem here. So I wanted to find out what it was before anybody else figured it out. Because in those days they could lock you up sooner than look at you if you were different in any way. If your parents could not control you, then off you went. I know a number of women my age who were totally institutionalized as the result of being locked up. My father tried to lock me up. I went out the window.

How old were you?

T: Oh, by then I was 17. No, I was older. All right, my checkered life. I went to college. That son of a bitch would not sign any of the papers, you know. But believe it or not, despite being drunk as a skunk through half of my junior and senior years in high school, I graduated with good enough grades to be accepted—not at the school of my choice but at a school which allowed me to work—and I got somebody else to sign the papers. Dear old Dad would never sign the papers because he did not believe in education for women. So I went to Goddard, and I was thrown out of college.

For?

T: Oh, what a funny question! [*Laughs*]

Well, I doubt that it was for low grades.

T: Yes, but you know, it was really weird because they never said it. I was thrown out twice. When I was finally summarily thrown out, definitively, it was because the college reserved the right to ask any student to leave for any reason. They never absolutely defined it until I was gone. Then they held an assembly for the student body, and they said, "This is why."

And they never said, "You are queer, so we are kicking you out"?

T: No. Not to me.

But they held an assembly after you were kicked out and they said, "She was queer"?

T: Yes.

So they didn't try to keep it quiet?

T: No. Actually, I was framed. OK, I had been involved with another undergraduate woman during my freshman year. And the following year—after I got kicked out the first time, during my freshman year—I went back and promised that I would try to keep my nose clean and what have you. You know, play the game. That was the worst problem I had in life—learning how much of the game I had to play in order to live the life I wanted to live. You know, how much before they would leave me the hell alone.

Anyway, so I went back, and one night I found a freshman in my closet, for God's sakes.

What an appropriate place.

T: What an appropriate place, yes indeed! Well, I wasn't that interested in her in the first place because I eventually was sleeping with the president of the government association in the seniors' suite, so why should I mess with a freshman? We don't need to go into that. But anyway, this freshman eventually ended up with my friend Ginny, and I do not know what happened, but it was something disastrous. I don't know what Ginny did to her, but the girl went out and got pregnant to prove to herself—to her parents or who the hell knows what—that she really wasn't queer. This is what you did. This is what people still do. You know, we prove that we're normal by going out and having a kid. Whoopee-do. And her parents were absolutely hysterical at the fact of this whole scenario, and they wanted to crucify the college. And the college, therefore, wanted to crucify whoever it was who was responsible for getting this girl so upset that she went out and slept with the first guy who passed by and got pregnant.

What had happened was that Ginny's roommate, Marty— Martha, a straight—knew that Ginny was involved with this girl. How could she not? And she told the administration that I had been the culprit. Months after I had been turned out, I wrote to her and said, "How come when they asked you, you said it was me and not Ginny?" And the answer was because Ginny was a senior and would not have graduated had they known. Ginny's father was putting her through too. But Ginny was her friend, and I wasn't—and that's what it boiled down to.

They just took her word for it?

T: Yes.

And you did have that history.

T: Yes, I had the history! Indeed, I did have the history. [*Laughs*] But it was more than that. Because in my freshman year when I got into trouble, I'd had a little encounter with the dean—her name was Phyllis, but we sort of referred to her as "Syphilis"; It seemed like a reasonable extrapolation. And she's giving me a straight-faced lecture—"We don't do that kind of thing!" You know, blah, blah, blah. And I said, "You're a helluva one to talk!" I don't remember what her name was, the head of the phys ed department, but they were obviously a couple. I should not have said that. It did not endear her to me. So she was perfectly happy, regardless of what

Marty had said, to put it on me because I represented a danger to her. But I was too young and stupid to realize that.

In many ways, you see, I was well ahead of my years, and in other ways I was just absolutely stupid and naive. I truly believed in fairness, you see. Justice and what have you. So, I came out of it not trusting anybody; isn't that a wonderful way to live?

It is ironic that your betrayal was assisted by another lesbian.

T: Yeah, these things happen. [*Laughs*]

Do you think that was commonplace for that time?

T: I think it's commonplace in this time. It's known as covering one's tail.

Once you realized, "Oh, this is who I am," and you began hearing terms such as "prevert" and queer, did you think of yourself in some kind of a twisted way. Or did you know enough to say, "No, it's those people who are cracked"?

T: No. When you were picked off the street—and this went on into the '60s—guilty or not guilty, you knew you were guilty. You didn't know what in the hell you were guilty of, but you knew you were guilty! When the laws were set up so that you could be locked up, committed long-term, just because you were there—not because you did anything, but just because of what they thought you had done—you knew that there was something wrong with you because the world couldn't work that way. That made no sense. That was not rational. Now that I'm old and gray, I understand the world is not rational. It *does* work that way.

How did you deal with those feelings of inferiority, of being sick and wrong?

T: One thing I have never done is feel inferior. I may have felt different and queer, but I have never felt inferior. It is something innate, which is probably my salvation. Because I come from a generation that says, "Well, I got married because I had to; they made me." You couldn't get a job, you couldn't do this, you couldn't do that. Well, hell! I did! You see? And I was very proud, down the road, not just about being gay, but in life in general. And I opened doors. I proved that I could, and therefore women can. And I am very pleased to report that in most of the jobs that I had it took two people to replace me. That just tickles the hell out of me, by God! That will show the sons of bitches!

And let me say this—it was tough for women to find work in those days. On an application, I always just signed my initial, "T. Genovese." That was the only way that you could get a job. It wasn't exactly subterfuge. You couldn't go in and say, "I am a woman seeking work!" It didn't work. You could not be a woman seeking work; you could be a *me* seeking work. You see? You could be an *initial* seeking work. But it was tough to be a *woman* seeking work.

After World War II, when women went back to their homes, was it doubly hard to find work at that point?

T: Oh, yeah. There were no jobs available, except in the secretarial fields. I wanted to go to Cornell University, and I certainly had enough credentials, grades, and what have you, and I was accepted. Despite everything, I was accepted at Cornell. So I wrote them, and I said, "Well, I will need work. What can you do for me?" And they wrote back and said, "There is no work on campus for women—unless you have exceptional skills in the secretarial area, there is no work, period." And this was a number of years after the War—1950. But this is what caught the women up short. They had been quite competent, quite skilled, doing very technical work in the Army, doing very technical work outside of the Army—blue collar, engineering, all this sort of stuff—and all of a sudden [to be told], "Go home and put on a frilly dress and play stupid because the men are coming home." That did not go over very well. So a number of them passed. Redsie I told you about.

My greatest jolt was the first time I saw a woman in total drag in New York. I must have been 16, 17. We're talking three-piece suits now. You could not tell! These were women who were dressed to the teeth as men, not just dressed like men. Profoundly impressive. Shortly after that you could become a "Smith College graduate school hockey team player." I've gotten a lot of teasing around here because of this vernacular, but this is what we knew them as—"the white-hockey-jacket crowd from the Sisters' colleges." And they had private clubs in New York, so they didn't have to go to the bars and drink. So, they didn't play in our yard, but they were there. And since they had money, class, and what have you, they did not suffer the egregious offenses.

So the women who might have gone to just a regular bar or café were typically working-class women?

T: No, not necessarily just working-class women. It would be women who did not have enough connections to be invited into the clubs. They could, in fact, be college graduates, but if they were not invited, they could not go. They would not even know where the club was. I mean, this is taking sorority a step higher. [*Laughs*]

Where else could you possibly meet women if you didn't meet them in a private club or in a bar?

T: We recognized each other more easily then than we do now— but we were scared. For instance, when we were selling Christmas trees for the church one year, a couple of women—that's two women together—they were out in public together. You didn't do this casually unless you were obviously mother and daughter or possibly sister and sister, but even that, not often. And I remember [my girlfriend and I] said to each other, "I bet they are." And we gave them extra greens with their tree and said, "Call us if you need more." And they called us. "Do come over for dinner." And they did.

In New Jersey I sang with the Sweet Adelines, an equivalent of a barbershop quartet. And I'm sitting there in barbershop, and I hear this big butch-lookin' woman coming in second bass. And I said, "God, you know she's got to be." [*Feminine voice*] "Oh, do you really think so, dear?" "Yeah, she's really got to be. We can take a chance on her." "Oh, all right. Let's invite her over." So [my girlfriend and I] invited her over. You know, with head in hand, because you could be crucified if you called out someone who wasn't. So we said, "Did you know that we were close? Um, we sort of felt that maybe you were..." [*Basso profundo*] "Me? Oh, my God! No! I'm not one of them! Oh, no!" And she left.

And we said, "Oh, shit. We've done it now." A couple days later she calls. She says, "I need to talk to you. Can you come over to my house?" So my girlfriend goes over, and the woman, Brandi, opens the trunk of her car, and inside the trunk is every cheap gay novel that has been printed in the past ten years. Now this is before *Beebo Brinker*, before Ann Aldrich. These are [the type where] the guy always gets the girl. These women were nothing like [lesbians in reality]. I read them. You know, because they were the only things available. But they were nothing like me. I didn't know who the hell they were writing about, but they sure as hell weren't like me—I always got the girl! [*Laughs*]

So anyway, that pretty well killed Brandi because obviously, if she's got this trunk load of books that she wants us to get rid of for her, then that means that she's one of us. So we took her into the bars.

And she kept these books in the trunk because...?

T: She was scared to take them anywhere else. Anyway, they were properly disposed of, which is, in a way, unfortunate. In context, it was certainly the smart thing to do then.

So, within a matter of weeks we had three couples. And this was how we did it. You met at people's homes. You went out to bars, whether you wanted to drink or not, because that was the only place you could go. How did we meet Big Jere? I don't know. Oh, we met Big Jere through Brandi. Everybody knew somebody who was or whom they thought was. And there were certain little [signals]. If you had a pinkie ring, well, then for sure. I mean, there was no discussion on this, dear. You obviously are. If you had been up to the Cape, and you were a teacher, you said, "Oh, I met you at a teacher's convention, didn't I dear?"

Would that be a euphemism, "Didn't I meet you at a teacher's convention on the Cape?"

T: Comparable. I mean, now you could say, "Oh, didn't I see you at the Kate Clinton concert?" That's the same thing.

Getting back to the Cape—because that was so wonderful before Kennedy and all the rest of them took over. Sunday afternoons in Provincetown we would all—all: gays, lesbians—go up to the Moors—the top floor of the Moors, the open, upstairs part. It could hold a couple hundred people, and we'd have a sing-along the entire afternoon. We'd eat lobster, and we'd sing. What did we sing? Not *gay* songs. There were no *gay* songs to sing. "Row, Row, Row Your Boat," "I've Been Working on the Railroad," "I Want a Girl Just Like the Girl...." You know; we sang. That was what we did, and it was wonderful. There was a camaraderie, which has since been totally missing. Today they talk about *the* community—*that* was community. You were safe. The guys, the gals—of all ages. There was a homogeneity, a homogeneous quality then that does not exist now and has not for a long time. And I miss it.

It seems, though, that one of the things that bound that community together was that intense level of fear.

T: Yes. But not of each other. And now there is fear of each other.

Why? What kind of fear exists now that didn't exist then?

T: OK. The fear then was from the outsiders. If you were involved with a married woman, you could be in a divorce suit–type thing. So it was the outsiders. The fear now is a social pressure kind of thing. The politically correct versus the non–politically correct—the separatists, the things that the separatist women do to the straight women, among others. Just absolutely beyond belief! You know, "Oh, you've brought a baby to a music festival? Well, screw you, lady. We're going to throw rocks at your tent all night!" Gimme a break. We're not like that.

I don't know where these people are coming from. We always trekked with the underdog. No matter who the hell it was, we fought for everybody's rights! Everybody's rights! Black, white, green—I don't care. And now it's all this little factionalized thing. "If you don't play the game our way, you're not welcome here." I find that totally as frightening as I did before. At least we knew the rules then. You knew what you could and couldn't do. Now you can't tell by looking who's what or who's going to do what to you. Unbelievable.

I guess this is where I have the advantage because I don't give a shit. But I feel so badly for these young mother types—whether they have conceived the child as a lesbian couple or in a marriage situation with a male partner. We're not getting into the pros and cons of the nobility of this or anything, but if they go to a music festival which is advertised as a music festival for women, not a lesbian-only closed shop, and they're hassled there, I take exception to that. Because they sure as hell—if they are married, they're having a problem just being there. You know, they have gone through something just to get there. And if they're not married, they're breaking ground—whether it's good or ill, I can't tell, but I'm not about to dump on them. I may have personal feelings, but I'm sure as hell not going to [dump on them]. So, we are not being as charitable to each other as we used to be to everyone—not just to each other, but to everyone.

To everyone who may have been different.

T: Exactly. The gays were in the forefront of the civil rights, the black marches in the South, because there was a feeling of rapport. Because they were being dumped on by the same people who were dumping on us.

Let me go back to where you were saying that it was so much easier to recognize a lesbian when you knew the rules. It is so much easier when you have rules of any kind.

T: There were definitions, yes. If you had the pinkie ring. It used to be you could do the same thing with earrings for the guys, but now you can't because all the guys are wearing earrings.

And I also—and this is a very personal thing—keep running into women who look me straight in the eye and say, "Well, I'm a lesbian by conscious decision." To which I must say, "Give me a break!" I mean, this is the biggest crock of shit I have ever in my life heard. "It's a political statement; it's got nothing whatever to do with being a lesbian." There's a woman down in Northampton, Mass., who drives me up a wall. She says, "I just can't imagine how anyone can have sex with another woman." But she's a lesbian, by God. She'll tell you she is. But she cannot imagine having sex with another woman.

Well, there's something incongruent about that.

T: Well, I think so, yes. [*Laughs*] But you see, there is a whole flock of them there, and they are "gay by conscious decision," and there is no problem in their own minds with this setup. And I am of the Joan Nestle School, and the Joan Nestle school says it's about sex, dear. You see? That is it. So being a lesbian nowadays is a political statement as much as a reality. I would hate to tell you how many women that are essentially gay women, lesbian women, occasionally come to me—you know, Big Mama, what the hell—and their problem is, "Well, I've been going with her for three months now, and she won't let me touch her." There's a whole flock of them out there. They want to run around and be with the women and the crowd, but about sex its, "Oh, God, don't touch me. What are you doing? Oh! What are you doing!" [*Laughs*] It's terrible. There is fear there, you see, because theoretically this is another lesbian, but actually it isn't. Now, my response to that is just to say, "Yeah, I'd love to come to dinner at your house, but that's it." And just stay the hell away from it. Because, like I say, there is an element of fear here—getting interested in, involved with. I don't want to beat my head against the wall, pursuing a goal that isn't there. At least, you know, when we were queer, we were *queer*! By God, I am queer! Are you queer? That's nice dear! But now, [*primly*] "I am a lesbian by conscious decision." That's nice, but play with yourself, and leave me the hell alone! [*Laughs*]

Is it your view that lesbianism is innate; you're born with it?

T: I think so. But I think also it's a continuum.

Do you consider yourself butch?

T: Yes.

But you mentioned to me over the phone that you enjoyed cooking. I thought that was supposed to be a femme activity?

T: Oh, no. That's not true. Most butches are excellent cooks. Most butches traditionally are excellent cooks by default. Whether it was default in the home is a moot point. It was in mine. I was the one who ended up doing the cooking. But if you were involved with a woman who was working in a woman's job and, therefore, bringing in the money, and you couldn't get a job because you wouldn't play the stupid game, you cooked. I'm sure you've heard that one before.

Yes. If you were going to define butch, how would you define it?

T: It's a state of mind.

OK. So it's not about what you would wear.

T: No. Well, partly. Your state of mind prohibits you from wearing some clothes in seriousness. You can wear them in drag funness. I stopped traffic in Livingston, N.J., one night—no, it was Irvington, N.J., one night at a four-way stop, well-lit, on Halloween, because I was dressed in a black, chic, flowing gown.

It's a state of mind. It's an attitude. It dictates how you walk, talk, think, and respond. It therefore, yes, has to do with dress. Because I personally do not feel comfortable in a dress or in anything fluffy and frilly. I don't know how I look. I have never known how I looked in whatever I wore, but I always felt that I didn't look right except in strictly tailored business suits, Pendleton suits and things like that, when I was working. You know, and other than that, jeans.

Well it is much more complicated now because today you can find a woman in work boots and overalls, and she may be perfectly straight.

T: Yes, and today you can go to work in anything. When I was working—and I was working pretty high-class, ground-floor computer stuff—you wore heels. You were supposed to be properly attired. Women always wore proper dresses, proper suits.

So a woman today might be decked out in what might, decades past, have been considered very butch attire, but in reality be quite femme.

T: There were always [women like that]. This is why I say it's a state of mind. There has always been a great difference between what you were to the public's eye and what you were in the bedroom. Because I have known a number of women that you'd say, "My God, total butch, *stone* butch—all down the line." But no, no, not at all. And there was a woman who just died a couple of years ago who was known as the epitome of stone butch. Well, not with me she wasn't. So I don't know, you know, what determines it. You dress how you feel comfortable, what feels right for you. Your mannerisms, how you feel comfortable, what feels right to you. But you can be a real pussycat on your own time. I do not subscribe to the [idea] that a butch must be totally hard and masculine.

Were there conventions that you followed?

T: I've had problems with women who did not want to be treated like women. As far as I'm concerned, a woman should like to be treated like a woman should like to be treated. And if she doesn't, why, that's her problem.

How is it to be "treated like a woman"?

T: I tend to be very deferential and hold doors and things like that, which is very passé, and the feminist movement does not like it. But I like it, you see, and I respect a woman who likes it. But I

spent the whole early feminist movement being madder than hell
at the feminists because they were dumping on women. They
were dumping on mothers. They were dumping on the "normals,"
which I'm sure was a reactionary thing, getting back at. But still,
it was stupid—"If you don't leave your husband and kids—after a
while, who wouldn't?—and find yourself..." These women had
not *lost* themselves. This was just who they were and what they
wanted to do, and to convince them otherwise struck me as the
height of cruelty. And there were even women who said, "Well,
you only *think* you're straight. You have to try sleeping with a
woman as well as sleeping with men before you know what you
are." No, no, no, no. Lesbians really racked up on it, you know.
[*Laughs*] I did not like that because in my world, you see, you fall
in love, and then you act upon it. You don't fall in *bed*. And yet,
that was what they were doing. All for the sake of a warped philosophy that made absolutely no sense to me.

What can I tell you? I start out being a wrong figure in the
straight community, and then I end up being a wrong figure in
the gay community. So you just say, "I am what I am." And I said
that before Harvey Fierstein ever came up with the thought. I
don't call him on plagiarizing; that's cool. [*Laughs*]

*You had said when we talked on the phone the first time that you had
always led a double life.*

T: I have *always* led a double life. I've always led a double life
because I cannot imagine being just a lesbian—and there's an
awful lot of them, in the East especially, who are so concerned
with being lesbians and about getting their lesbian credentials,
they will not work for "the man," they will not do this, that, and
the other thing because it is offensive to their values.

They had a meeting one night, and they said, "Let us discuss
our lesbian values." And I said, "Well, what is a lesbian value?"
"Well, that's what we're here to decide." And I said, "Well, I have

these human values, and I get along very well as a human being." Oh, these women drive me up a wall!

No, I think it's a very sterile life if you try and live totally as a lesbian. In academia is the only place I know that you can probably do it without being supported by "the man," you know, as a welfare-type case, which is beneath my dignity. I don't know how it is on yours. But I have never had a trouble with men. I *like* men. I like men as people. I like men to talk to, you know, to *be* with. I have absolutely no interest in them sexually. I have absolutely no interest in going anyplace with them or doing anything with them, but I will be very glad to sit down and talk politics with them. I won't talk sports because I don't care about it much, you know, but I think I have more in common with the average man than I do with the average woman because that's just how my interest has developed.

I have lived in the straight world. I serve the straight world, and I always have, in some capacity or other. I don't do it as a cover; I do it because that is part of me. Part of me needs to be satisfied in things that are not available within the gay community. As I say, I am me. Now, I have been hassled more by the gays than I have been by the straights. The straights, I think, are absolutely priceless because—I would say at least 75%, and possibly 99%, of the people in this town know that I'm gay. "We don't talk about it, dear." Now I'm told that I'm supposed to carry around a picket sign that says, "I'm Gay; Is That OK?" I don't care if it's OK or not. You see, I am. I am. I have no reason to put these people or anyone else that I know up against the wall and say, "I'm gay; you deal with it!" Why should they have to deal with it? It's got nothing to do with them. But the result is very interesting and downright comical sometimes.

I have a friend in Boston. She and I were involved for a period of time, and we're still best of friends. And she would come out here sometimes for R and R, and we'd play cards with some of the women in town. And then I got a new girlfriend. And when [my new girlfriend] came to visit, the gang would get together and play cards. And then my girlfriend went on vacation to Alaska, and she came back with some neat pictures. Anyway, we're passing the pictures around, and my friend, Betsy, looks at them and passes them to Barbara. And Barb is at the head of the table, and she looks at them and says, "This doesn't look like the same woman who used to come and play cards with us." And before I could respond, Betsy said, "Oh, no, dear. That was the *old* one. This is the *new* one." And Barb said, "Oh. O-o-oh!" You see, obviously [they know], but "we just don't talk about it, dear." But it is fun. It is. And it's nice because I know that the people in town would go to bat for me, and numbers of them, in fact, have done so, you know, in general, whenever anyone comes up with a snide remark.

And let me say this about Betsy—Betsy has been, I think, in love with me since I moved to town. She writes me love notes! But then she always denies that's what they are. It's hysterically funny. She'll write, "You're wonderful. I'm so glad I know you. You make my life complete. I wish we could do more together." She usually doesn't like the women that I go out with. She may like them, but she wishes they weren't there. You get the very definite impression that she wishes they weren't there.

For some 20-odd years this has continued?

T: Yes. And it has been a hoot and a half because obviously she's straight. And she'll write me these flowery things, and I'll say, "Betsy, you forgot to sign it. *You* wrote me that, didn't you?" And she'll say, "Yes, but don't let it go to your head!" [*Laughs*] It's absolutely comical.

Is Betsy married?

T: Well, no, she's widowed. And she went traveling across the country with a gentleman, and he came back and turned her in for another woman. She said, "I never have been any good at sex." And I was just waiting for her to say, "Teach me, O Great White Mother," but she didn't.

I guess for lesbians it's getting easier because more women look like lesbians—or what we stereotypically think of as a lesbian look. But for our gay brothers—or for any man—sadly, it's still not acceptable to wear a dress.

T: No, and yet, one of my best buddies, Allen, he's 79. He's in the hospital, and I don't think he's going to make it, and he has been an out queer for so many years. And his persona is Miss Sophie Tucker. He is the incarnation of Miss Sophie Tucker. A short and stocky little guy. Allen—Sophie Tucker—lives in public housing in a nearby town. And the ladies down there—of course they don't know that he's queer—the ladies down there give him their old gowns so he will be properly dressed for his performances in a local senior's chorus. [*Laughs*] And I have never, never seen this man perform in the chorus in slacks. He always wears a dress. He may not be Sophie Tucker, but he always sings wearing a dress. And he is always one of the female chorus. He has a lovely tenor voice. So he is being well taken care of—in drag—by the older ladies, who do not know he is gay, of course.

He just likes these dresses.

T: Yes. And he looks so good in them, dear! "It's just stunning on you, Allen. Please keep it!" [*Laughs*] But I am quite comfortable with this, and this has been fairly historical. The older generation is less uptight. The people who are 60 and older are less uptight than the people who are 40 to 60, who are more uptight than the people who are younger. So the older people accept gay, but they don't talk about it. They know we're gay! What's the big deal?

Why should they make a production of it? They don't want to bother or to offend anybody; it's just "we like and accept you." I don't ask them what they do in bed, and they don't ask me what I do! It's as simple as that.

It's the whole idea of, "To each his own."

T: Yeah.

You mentioned to me on the phone that 99% of older lesbians won't tell their stories or won't talk. I certainly know this to be true.

T: We got 'em in nursing homes now. OK. And I've done a little with these people that are in nursing homes or public housing. And I know they're gay, and they know that I know they're gay, and they get hysterical that I'm going to tell someone that they're gay. Because they have spent so long playing the game and accommodating and being afraid that someone would tell. And if someone tells, they know they'll be alone because everyone will leave them. And it has happened this way. And these are women who are not sure of who they are themselves. Most of them have married, have children, have grandchildren. Theresa, I had her for a while in a group we set up for older gays and lesbians. And she said, "I can't come to the meetings anymore. I don't want you to send me the newsletter. Because there's a gay couple down on the corner, and they have a child, and I said to my daughter, "Oh, isn't that cute, and what a lovely baby!" And my daughter said, "They're queers! If you ever have anything to do with those queers, you'll never see your grandson again!"

Now, this may have been a throwaway line, but Theresa didn't want to risk it. People will come once and know we're there. They will call on the phone. They don't want to go in public. They don't want to be seen with us. I can list the names of women. There's one woman, a very out lesbian. She has probably been in every civil rights movement, march, protest that ever was. She still is. And she's up in public housing, and she has a habit of going up to people and saying, "I'm a lesbian; want to talk about it?" [*Laughs*] I think that's fine, but the other gay women up there are having a raining shit fit. When they see her, they'll turn and go around. They will skip meals rather than eat in the same dining room with her. Because they are terrified that she will come up to them and say, "Oh! I saw you at the showing of *Desert Hearts*." It's sheer fear on their part. I can't advise that these women rock that boat because their whole life has been built around accommodating. They don't know how *not* to accommodate. It's too late to start rebuilding.

I'm sort of in that situation myself. But the terror of it is, the older you get, the more you like to reminisce. Now, who you gonna reminisce with? You go into an old folks home, you go in for just short-term. [*In a sweet little old lady voice*] "Hello, dear. My name is Mildred. I have 17 grandchildren—four boys, six girls, and the rest are undecided. How many grandchildren do you have?" What do you say? [*In a gruff voice*] "I don't have any because I'm a lesbian." [*Laughs*] So, you cannot cut older people off from what they have known.

We have a new generation coming up, and they are going to have to come up with strictly gay and lesbian nursing homes and things because [elders] don't know how to think about these things; they don't even *want* to think about them.

I can understand that in a sense. That group of much older gay people who are in nursing homes already have so many of their rights gone.

T: Exactly. And they will deny it. And this is their right. They will deny it because they think it's all a trick.

I imagine that elders believe that they have a lot to lose after a lifetime of hard work. There's a lot at stake.

T: Absolutely. Absolutely. What am I going to do? This is my home. And I have stood up for things in which I believe, you know. And everybody knows me as the—what is it?—"prominent local eccentric," and I like that title. I could live as the prominent local eccentric until I'm a hundred, you see? It's much better than "fucking queer." And we have a lot of fundamentalists in this town; some of them are my friends. But you know, "We love the sinner, and we hate the sin." But as long as nobody says, "Well, let's go out and throw stones at her." They're very protective of me. I'm the "prominent local eccentric," and I love it.

Well, that's one of the historic euphemisms for lesbian—"eccentric," "athletic."

T: Oh, yes, absolutely—"athletic." And there's also "mannish."

How about role models, lesbian role models that we were talking about. Roller Derby.

T: Oh, yeah! Tuffy Brasuhn! Gerry Murphy! Goddamn! Of the Jersey Jolters. Gerry was married, but I'm not sure if that was for real.

Billie Jean King was married.

T: Figure out what side of the bed you're on or get out of here.

Now we're discovering these duplicities.

T: But then we didn't. No, no, no. My God! Heresy!

As I told you, when I was growing up in the '60s, there was one lesbian that I could identify, and she was a Roller Derby skater, and I thought she was hot stuff.

T: I'm sure she was. My goodness, yes!

But you had to know that she was a butch lesbian; she couldn't have passed for anything else.

T: Well, it's only butch because in *your* mind that is butch. She was a very *strong* woman. I mean, if you're wearing a roller derby outfit, you can't say that is butch. That is a Roller Derby outfit.

Well, I saw her offtrack…

T: At least with a small cigar, a Tiparillo?

And I will say with some certainty that she was butch. She wore hopsack Levi's trousers, penny loafers…

T: Well, of course.

White socks…

T: White! No! No! No! Oh, I'm sorry! That's against the rules. You know that!

No, I didn't know that.

T: Femmes wore white socks; butches wore colored socks. To this day, I have a hell of a time putting on white socks. My girlfriend says, "It's all right, dear; that's passé." I have very few pair of white socks, but I have an entire collection of black socks, navy socks…

Brown socks.

T: No, not anymore. I don't go for brown.

Now, she also wore a man's sport shirt—short sleeve, button-down...

T: Yes! Of course! They wear better, and they have two pockets.

And she wore a man's windbreaker and had a DA.

T: Of course! And men's pants wear better and fit better than women's. I mean, "We hold these truths to be self-evident." I cannot wear women's clothes. The sleeves are too short, the butt in the pants is too big. I just cannot do it! And they've got this concept of "waist." Give me a break! I mean, I can tell you what size I am—I'm a 36-28. You go into a women's store and ask for 36-28, and they just look at you.

And they say, "Two, four, six, eight, ten, 12, or 14?"

T: I don't know. And that's getting funny at this age and stage of my life. I haven't the vaguest idea. I also wear a men's size 8½ shoe. Well, that translates into a 10½ women's, approximately. Do you think you can get 10½ women's? And it's so stupid. I mean, give me a break. I mean, if you're talking high heels—stilettos or something like that, which I did wear when I had to but not very much—then you can see some discernible difference. But if you're talking loafers, sneakers, and what have you, a shoe is a shoe, for God's sake!

But I'm quite sure she was pretty butch—minus the white socks. Now I may have to call the whole thing into question.

T: Well, no, the white socks may just been because she realized that the dye in dark socks is bad for your feet. And if she had foot problems from skating, we can forgive her for wearing white socks. But, oh, my God! My dear! You would take a terrible amount of ribbing wearing white socks!

This skater was very visible at a time when I just didn't see that many women whom I could identify. I did see men.

T: Women always had uniforms, and the men didn't. That just occurred to me. In the late '40s, I wore a silk dress shirt, a man's dress shirt, a burgundy velour sweater, black wool slacks in winter, khakis in summer. That was *the* uniform—black slacks, sweater, and loafers. The shirt could change. That was pretty much, universally, the uniform—a man's shirt, men's slacks, and in the summer if you wore white, that was kind of show-offy, so you wore khaki. But powder blue, pink? No. Not even femmes wore that.

And the femme uniform? Was there such a thing?

T: No. They had looser dress requirements. Most of them wore slacks. I liked them in dresses. I don't know why. Now, why did butches wear what they wore? I don't know. It was a statement of some kind. I'm not convinced it was emulating a man—except for safety's sake because you had to. It was just, "I'm more comfortable this way; make something of it. If you don't like it, tough darts!"

Earlier, we were talking about young lesbians "pushing people's noses in being gay." You know, "I'm here, I'm queer, get over it!" But do you ever think that this higher visibility is good? Does it ever give you a greater sense of security?

T: Oh, no! It gives me a greater sense of fear. Because they're mucking it up for us. All right, this is my attitude, and this is the attitude of an old fruit. My attitude is that I have lived a reasonably good life. I have served the community—the gay community, the straight community, all of them. This is not a super moral issue, but this is just a personal feeling that we should be here to accomplish something for others and not just for ourselves, and the young people are all shot with "look at me, here I am, do for me." This is totally contrary to my life. Now, I have always tried to help. I'm an MFDG—a mother-fucking do-gooder—what can I tell you? But it was something that was ingrained as a function of time. It's something that came out of the Depression. It's something that came out of how things were before World War II. A feeling of "we're all in this together." And I need that for my soul's sake, and I think that a lot of the older people do—a feeling of community. I don't find that in the lesbian community. I *do* find it in this little community; I am part of this town. I belong here. The first place in my entire life where I felt I belonged. I do not feel that I belong in the lesbian community because it's too factionalized.

I have a lot of friends down there. I have more friends in the gay community than I have in the straight community, but they are acquaintance-type things. But I feel safer here, a part of something.

I'll tell you a funny story about that. We had a problem one year with a senior English teacher at the high school coming on to the boys. And, in fact, quite openly sleeping with one of the senior boys. So, it caused quite a major scandal. And I thought it was totally inappropriate. So the superintendent of the schools, who knew I was gay, formed an ad hoc committee to see what ground rules we could set up governing teacher behavior on school time.

"Rule Number One: Do not sleep with the students."

T: Exactly! [*Laughs*] But there was nothing in the teacher contract. And we had to have something that could be agreed upon. And the ad hoc committee consisted of three gay women and three ultraconservative men. Now, we knew that they were conservative; they did not know that we were gay. *We* knew we were gay. One of whom was a retired editor from *Newsweek* magazine; one of whom was a sweet woman who had retired from the local school system. You know, her friend. A couple of old maids living together—"Isn't that sweet, dear." And then there was yours truly. We go through this, and we come up with what we consider a workable document. And in the last session, Cynthia, the *Newsweek* one, turns to Joe Stevens, who was the most supercon- servative of the conservative men, and said, "You know, we haven't mentioned anything about women in there." And Joe says, "What do you mean?" "You know, lesbians." "Oh," he says, "we don't have to worry about that. We can spot one a mile away; we'll just never hire one." We didn't tell him how many of us were there at that point in time.

So you think that it's a more powerful position—just quietly infiltrating?

T: Oh, absolutely. I do. I firmly believe it because I have proven beyond just about anybody's doubt that we can be, I can be, I am and have been a functioning member of the greater community, a decent human being doing for the town, doing for the people. You got a problem? Trudy will help you. Your husband beat you up? Trudy's is a safe house. Just the fact of being here. I wrote the bicentennial play for this town. I was one of three people writ- ten up in the bicentennial report as "an outstanding citizen of our community." And I love it. Because they see me as a human being, and I *am* a human being. I am a functioning human being who happens to be gay. I am not a gay woman who may or not be human. And to me that is very important.

Valerie Taylor
Tucson, Arizona

"I'm a Quaker, in case you haven't met an old dyke who writes lurid tales and is a Quaker," says Valerie Taylor, 77, extending her hand in welcome and ushering me into her half of a small cement-block duplex in a slightly tattered section of Tucson.

When I arrive Taylor's in the midst of making rice soup and immediately asks if I'm hungry. "Feeding people is my thing," she announces, plying me with soda crackers, cookies, and tea the moment I am seated. Returning to her tiny Pullman-style kitchen, she stirs the lumpy soup and frowns. "Well, this may not be palatable, but it will be edible," she says, returning to the table, where she'll hold forth for six hours—pausing only for eyedrops that keep incipient glaucoma at bay—with the story of how a mild-mannered girl from Aurora, Ill., emerged in the 1950s and early '60s as an out writer of lesbian pulp fiction and a founding member of the homophile Mattachine Society in Chicago.

Taylor's two-room apartment is lined with books and more books: volumes of poetry, turn-of-the-century Victorian tearjerkers, labor history, and novels by Hemingway and Gertrude Stein and Henry Miller—all arranged alphabetically, even in the bathroom. She estimates more than 3,000 books are stacked neatly on shelves. An original watercolor by Miller, painted during his years at California's Big Sur, hangs on one wall. Her writing desk sits in a corner against a window. A technophobe, Taylor, even here eschews most modern conveniences, sharpening her pencils with a simple razor blade. "My son says I get out my castration impulses that way," she says with a straight face she terms her "mandarin" expression.

Her story includes a bitter marriage, motherhood, divorce, and a hardscrabble single mother's existence, supporting her three children, in turn, as a switchboard operator, editorial assistant, editor, ad copy writer, advertising manager, door-to-door magazine saleswoman, confessions writer, and novelist. Along the way, damn public opinion, she came out as a lesbian. As Taylor herself says, "I didn't have time to worry about what people would think. I was going full speed ahead, trying to support my three sons."

Interviewed January 1990

Pouty Vixens and Sweater Girls: Confessions of a Lesbian Pulp Fiction Writer

Didn't most lesbian-themed pulp novels of the 1950s and early 1960s typically end with someone jumping out of a window?

V: Some of them did, yes. I wrote my books in the days when good lesbian novels were very scarce. I didn't set out to write good books but books in which people acted authentically.

I remember reading a particularly desperate little book by Ann Aldrich called We Two Won't Last.

V: I've read that. She wrote three or four lesbian novels. And she always said she was a lesbian, but we never knew if she loved us or hated us because so much of the time her people were so miserable and presented in such an unfavorable light. I used to know Ann Aldrich's real-life name, but any name you're known by is your real name. I wasn't born "Taylor." I was born Velma Tate, and that's still the name I vote with, sign petitions with. I kept my initials thinking that if I ever had anything monogrammed, it wouldn't be a problem. I chose "Valerie" because it means brave. I had a closet full of those books when I left Chicago, and I gave them all away.

At any rate, I wanted to do a book about people who had families and jobs and allergies—whatever real human beings have. And the first one I wrote, *Whisper Their Love,* had a young woman who fell in love with a man at the end and changed her evil ways, more or less. The evil was implied; I didn't say it. And the second one was *The Girls in 3B.* Three country girls go to the big city—the big city being Chicago, of course. What happened to them—and what amuses me when I think about how much publicity there is now about incest and rape—is that one of the women had been raped by an uncle, I think—certainly not her father. And I was told that I couldn't have her raped or abused as a child by a blood relative. I couldn't put that on paper.

And what year was that?

V: It was 1959 or '60. She's the one who becomes the lesbian, partly because she is directed to it. You had to have some rationale for it like this traumatic experience.

Well, the same is true for your character Erika Frohmann, who in Journey to Fulfillment *is turned away from men as the result of her experiences in Steinhagen, a Nazi concentration camp.*

V: Yes, exactly. Except I also feel that she would have been a lesbian anyway, probably. At any rate, after all the other Erika books had been published—this is the first one in the narrative but nearly the last to be written—the first to be written was *World Without Men,* which I saw as Kate's story. And I invented Erika to solve Kate's dilemma, but then Erika sort of took me over. She is a very real person to me, and she has absolutely no origins anywhere as far as I know. She came out of my hot little head. She was born full-fledged—the way she looked, her old loden coat, everything. Her previous experiences. But this was the third of the Erika books to be published—written and published.

The love scenes in this book are quite explicit.

V: They were written before that was really permissible, much less popular.

Your books and most of the lesbian pulp fiction of that era have such melodramatic titles—Stranger on Lesbos, World Without Men. Did you title any of these?

V: I titled the first one *The Heart Takes Many Paths,* which was from an old Arabic proverb—I was the old Arab who made it up—

"The heart takes many paths in search of love." And it was Leona Nemler at Fawcett, a very good editor to whom I'm grateful, who insisted upon calling it *Whisper Their Love*. It was the time of the lavender half world and the secret lesbian world, and *Whisper Their Love* was published with a preface—or maybe it was a tailpiece—by some psychologist that nobody had ever heard of—I'm sure he was the office boy at the publishing house—saying, "Mothers, have your daughters read this book so they will not fall into the same sad misfortunes." I thought it was very funny. It was so obviously a security blanket sort of thing—"We're publishing this, but we're not really approving of it." I had put in years of writing confession stories, so this was a familiar gambit to me. It wasn't that sad a book. She *did* end up marrying a nice, young male doctor. I've been getting hell for it ever since from lesbians who say, "Why did you give that book a sad ending?" I didn't see it as a sad ending. She was a girl who had been pushed by circumstances into going briefly through a lesbian experience.

Who bought your books, and where did they buy them?

V: I think that a great many people bought them through legitimate bookstores. They were sold at Kroch's and Brentano's in Chicago. The first time I ever actually saw anyone buy a book of mine—you know, you think you're dropping it down a manhole— a young man in Kroch's and Brentano's paperback department in downtown Chicago bought it, picked it off the shelf and took it over to the desk to pay for it, and it was all I could do to keep from rushing up to him and thanking him, you know, shaking hands or something, but I managed not to.

But there were a lot of people. There were lonely lesbians who thought they were the only ones, and they used to write. Those letters were very appealing. They'd say, "I'm 45 years old, and I know I'm a lesbian, but I've never had a lover. How do you find anybody?" And they'd write to me through the publisher. You know, publishers are pretty good about forwarding mail, generally. Those I found very moving. Or young girls who'd ask, "How do I know whether I'm a lesbian or not?"

But a lot of men bought these books as pure wish-fulfillment stuff. And some of the lesbians in some of these books were just fantastic. They were husky butches, who, however, wore black lace underwear. There was one who thrust her arm into her lover's vagina up to the elbow. I've often thought, "Wouldn't it be interesting to meet a woman like that!" But I think that just about everybody bought gay books in the late '50s and early '60s because a lot had been written about them and people were curious. And a lot of women—housewives, nice housewives—would think, "Well what is this? What do they have, anyway, that makes them throw away marriage and motherhood and the right to wash the dishes and do the laundry forever?" And they would buy them and hide them. I know a lot of married women who bought them.

Given your subject matter, did you get much hate mail?

V: Very little, and when I did it was usually not hate in toto, but some little detail that would be objected to. Of course, I didn't have these up-to-the-elbow scenes, having been around and had a few lovers myself and being female myself. They were incredible, just incredible, and they were nearly all male written under female names, like Sylvia Sharon, who was a man writing in Chicago. His real name was Paul Little, and he claimed to have written over 60 lesbian pulp novels. Years later when I went to New York to see the people at Midwood Tower, who published a lot of his books, they said, "Oh, yes, oh yes, Paul's books. Sure. He sketches out a plot, and then our staff writes the book." And I'm sure a lot of the others did the same thing. These people wrote incredibly bad books. The women [in them] were all figments of imagination. Nobody has ever written one of my books except me. It may not be a good book, but it's mine. It's like, I may have a lousy personality, but it's my very own, and I'm not trading it in.

Were you actually the first woman to pen these books?

V: I don't know. You would think after *The Well of Loneliness* came out others would have written what was in their hearts to write, but of course Radclyffe Hall was a very special person. She was wealthy, had an independent income. She cross-dressed—we didn't call it that in those days. I don't think they called it anything in particular. It was a part of her aristocratic, exclusive, wealthy, and upper-class British "Stephen." And I don't think Americans wrote very much along those lines because they saw it as being a special kind of book. Except for Gale Wilhelm; she wrote two books, which were very, I thought, well done. Books that would have stood up at any time. They have been reprinted several times.

Your books' cover price was about 35 cents.

V: Oh, yes. My first book sold for 25 cents, and when they marketed the next one at 35 cents I was afraid that nobody would buy it, that nobody would put that extra dime down on a book that was going to be read and thrown away.

How many of these books were published?

V: Oh, God! There must have been hundreds, thousands, I suppose.

Let me read something to you. Here we have Peg in Journey to Fulfillment.

V: How could I forget Peg!

Peg brings Erika Frohmann out, and they've made love.

V: Peg was a nasty girl.

You say, "Outside the rain strummed steadily against the waiting ground, which lay like a woman, thirsty and open for love." That's wonderful!

V: Well, that's not bad! I'd forgotten I'd written that!

I read that paragraph five or six times alone.

V: Yes, well, Peg was all right, basically.

You mentioned that Rice and Beans, *your latest book, just came to you.*

V: That's the second time that happened. *Prism* came to me that way too.

Did these earlier books come to you that way?

V: No. I just had an inkling of an idea, and I sat down and started with page one, chapter one, and just wrote them through, and they developed, they incubated as I wrote. I think books usually do that. I never make anything formal like an outline, but sometimes I mull over a book and write little scraps of paper about it and put them in a cardboard box. I very seldom go back to read them, but writing them fixes them in my mind.

I've always lived, I may say, below the poverty line since I quit working, and I was in the publishing business before that, so you may know that I wasn't very rich. Publishing is ill-paid. And two years ago I decided that I would apply for food stamps. You can't live very well on social security. It's a rice-and-beans kind of income. So I went to a place that is described in the first chapter—they said it was an employment office, but it wasn't. It was the place where you go to get food stamps, the Department of Economic Security—and that's an oxymoron if I ever heard one.

At any rate, I went there with a nice Hispanic lady whom I met on the bus bench, and both of us were totally baffled by what we found. The DES gives a 36-page booklet, and one of the things they want to know is the names of everyone who lives in your building, even though you may not be related, and are any of them out on strike. Union busting. Definitely, Arizona is a non-union state. They have a right-to-starve law here. At any rate, when we came out, the Mexican lady who was with me, whom I'd never seen before or since, said, "They don't give you any dignity; that's what's the matter with these places."

So I came home with my 36-page booklet. You have to have receipts from your utilities, copies of your income tax returns. I haven't filed an income tax return since 1977 because I've never earned enough that I have to. I came home very downcast because, what am I going to do? I wouldn't have health care today except some of my friends pay toward it. I have ten friends who each put in $10 a month, and that pays for my HMO and my eyedrops and so on. [That night] I went to bed and slept soundly with all my worries, and in the morning when I woke up, I had this complete book with [the characters] Marty Brown and Thea Shuler, and the whole story beginning in the DES office. So I sat down, and I wrote it, and in six weeks I had written three drafts of it, including a final typing. And I was so tired that when I walked down the street I felt as if I were standing still and the houses were moving past. The other time, I went to sleep on a farm belonging to friends of mine in the Catskills in New York, and *Prism* came to me overnight, and I had the whole thing. But it took me a longer time to write it; I took my time.

Did you have any inkling when you were a teen or a young woman that you were a lesbian?

V: I don't think so. I always had crushes. Girls had crushes in those days on older girls, on teachers. You almost routinely fell in love with a teacher, but it was very—what shall I say? It was more nonsexual. It was an emotional attachment. You were romantically in love with somebody.

Did you have boyfriends?

V: I went with a nice Jewish boy, Sam Silvergilt, during college. This was Blackburn College, in 1935. I was in school, and nobody had any money. When my mother would write to me, I'd feel the envelope to see if she'd sewn a dime or a quarter into it—she'd take the paper and write the letter on it and then put the money in and stitch around it so it couldn't fall out of the envelope and get lost. If she sent the dime, I had money for notebook paper; otherwise I didn't. And at the beginning of the year, they had a big contest—big for a small town—an essay contest, and the people who wrote the best essays were given $5. Now $5 was *money* in those days. You could buy a dress and a pair of shoes for $5. So I went out for the "Why I Am Proud to Be an American"—ugh—contest, which the Daughters of the American Revolution—also ugh—were doing. And I won half of the prize, and Sam won the other half. He was a local boy; his father kept a little store there in the village. And they had a banquet, so you got a fancy meal out of it too. After eating in commons for a few weeks, that was something in itself.

We sat with the lady who was representing the DAR, and she didn't quite know what to do with Sam. I was a stranger—it was all right, but he was a local boy who was, after all, Jewish. I could have been too, for all she knew, could have been anything. I'm part Indian, as a matter of fact. So she was making polite conversation; she was being nice, and we were being nice. And she said, "I don't know if you young people can realize what it means to me to be an American, but I am a collateral descendant of Button Gwinette, who signed the Declaration of Independence. And Sam looked amiably at her—he was a short little guy, very sharp-looking—and he said, "Oh, I can understand that; I'm a collateral descendant of the guy who signed the Ten Commandments." I do love that! She just didn't know what to do.

But what I was going to say about prejudice cutting in all directions was that Sam's mother and grandmother were terrified that he was going to get involved with a Gentile. I mean, seriously involved—maybe he'd have to get married or something dreadful. And I had not realized. In my family there was no prejudice along any line, really. I hadn't realized that people on the other side are prejudiced too. Blacks, as a rule, don't want their kids marrying whites, or Caucasians—or didn't in those days, 'cause it creates all kinds of problems. The relatives get all chewed up about it, you know. If I'd have brought home a Jewish son-in-law for my mother, she'd have been delighted, but Sammy's family wouldn't have been happy.

Fortunately, there was never any question—we were good friends; we fought for top place in the freshman class that year. On noondays we'd buy a nickel sack of peanuts—if we had a nickel—go out to the Civil War cemetery, sit on a tombstone, and eat peanuts. That was a red-hot date when you didn't have any money. We never got serious about each other. He subsequently graduated from someplace else with honors, joined the Navy, and became a high-ranking naval hospital staff person at Bethesda. I should have wished I'd been a little more aggressive: I would have ended up with money, status—ugh, armed forces. But a nice boy.

And in fact, I made a very bad marriage when I was 25. I had three kids, one single and one pair of twins. And I never had an actual, overt lesbian relationship until after I'd gotten my divorce at the age of 40.

In what year were you married?

V: In 1939.

That's what young women did in those days.

V: Yes, that's what young women did, and my mother had impressed upon me that I was quite ugly because I have a spinal curvature, obviously. Nobody would ever want to marry me, and I did want to be married. I did want some love in my life and children. So I married the first man who seemed willing to be married. He turned out to be an alcoholic and eventually was on hard drugs. A very bad marriage. So, after 14 years of this I threw him out. I got my final papers a week before my 40th birthday.

That was very courageous.

V: Well, you do what you have to do. You reach a point of necessity. And he had been abusive to the children up to a point, and they were glad to see him go. They were 10 and 12, almost 11 and 13, so they were old enough to be pretty independent. And it wasn't easy.

That was the early '50s?

V: Yeah. In '53 I got my final decree. It was not easy, but we made it.

Had you been working all that time?

V: No. I taught country school for a year before I got pregnant. But there is no country school for a pregnant teacher. And I stayed at home because my husband, who also did not support us adequately, did not want me to work. He was a very neurotic—

excessively—almost psychotic man. He didn't want me to go any-where or do anything.

Things got worse and worse, and I knew I had to leave. One of my kids was in therapy, for which the school system paid. So I just went out and got myself a job. They said, "Can you use a PBX switchboard?" And I said, "Certainly." I didn't know what a PBX switchboard was. It was the old-fashioned kind where you push these buttons up and down instead of pushing in plugs. So I went to the public library, and sure enough, they had a very old man-ual on how to run a PBX switchboard. I went in on Monday morning and the man said this is so-and-so, and she's going to take a week to show you how to run everything. I don't do well with technology.

About three years ago, Jean Sirius, the poet, and her lover, Cara, sent me an electronic typewriter as a birthday gift, and I couldn't use it. The keys were too small—I would hit two keys with one finger. I couldn't change the ribbons; I couldn't change the correction tape. I traded it in on something else, and that didn't work. So I finally traded it in on this monstrosity, which is just like the one I had before, a nice old IBM Executive. We're very compatible. But some machines don't like me.

I tend to be animistic. You know, the Indians believe that everything has a spirit, and the spirit either does or doesn't like you, and if the spirit doesn't like you, you just avoid it as much as possible. If you have a kitchen knife, and it cuts you, you assume first that you were stupid and clumsy with it, and you become very careful. If it cuts you again, you get rid of the knife—that knife is inimical to you. That makes as much sense as anything else. So, I suspect some machines don't like me.

And you know I believe in thought transmission. Jean Sirius's lover has been suffering from a cancer of the sinus. And I think we had about 200 women all over the country mobilized to think about her. The Quakers say to hold her in the light—a nice phrase, I think—and send her healing thoughts. And she has come through. Now, don't tell me it was just an accident. People were loving Cara and sending her their thoughts.

That's rather like the way in which you received those stories.

V: Oh, sure. I think the Goddess gave them to me. You could say that they came out of my unconscious, but what is your unconscious? Freud's idea of the unconscious was purely mechanistic, but if you read Jung, for example, he believed in racial memory, a pool of information that people shared. And he was a hard-headed psychologist.

It's funny that we talk about the unconscious as an "it," but if we opened someone up surgically, what can we see?

V: There'd be no spirit, yet I believe that matter can't disappear. If matter can't be destroyed, how can spirit be destroyed? I don't know what happens to people when they die. Maybe they blend in with a great, huge something, but I do think that spirit is indestructible. But religion—that's another matter. I don't call myself religious, but I am very spiritual. Look at how the fundamentalists have sway over their people. Look at Jim Bakker. They're quite ignorant and money hungry. It's obvious that they're in it for money. My son heard that particularly obnoxious one, the one who said that if he didn't get $80,000—

Oral Roberts.

V: Right. God would take him up. You know, I said to [my son] Jim, "Why did no one call him up and say, 'Oh, Brother Roberts, you're a believer, a true believer! What you should want, more than anything in the world, is for God to take you home to heaven! Let's all kneel down and pray that the money doesn't come so that you can have that great joy and happiness of going to be with

God!'" But they didn't. The fools sent the money. [*Laughs*] And that seems, to most of us, so crude. And we may well say those are stupid, ignorant people. They have no background. They don't read anything, unless it's the usual magazines that tell you all the dirt, you know. They're quite fascinating. I buy them at the grocery store—the *Enquirer*, the *Examiner*, the *Star*—because they are just fascinating. I'm trying to write an article for one, but I haven't succeeded.

What would you write?

V: I don't know. I've been hoping to think of something suitable. Something with a little phony mysticism in it. It's a vagrant sort of thought. Alien abduction is very big now. Or very old or very young people who have children—"Seven-Year-Old Boy Impregnates Neighbor!" Of course, if the husband believes that, he'll believe anything. [*Laughs*].

We've gone all the way up to 1953.

V: Oh. Well, then I got this job. I had never actually had an active male lover. My husband was my first. I was one of those terribly good girls, which I think should probably be forbidden by law. On the other hand, you read Aldous Huxley, and you're not sure about total sexual freedom either. I had been very much in love with a woman who was a neighbor, but nothing ever came of it, nor did I really try to make anything come of it. I think for women loving women, the border is so imperfectly defined. There is more emotion. I'm not saying that there's less physical reaction, but—except for the young ones who are growing up with a more rational attitude—it's much easier to think, well, this is an emotional relationship rather than a genital one. The woman [Lillian Faderman] who wrote *Surpassing the Love of Men* points that out about some of those early relationships, the Boston Marriages. So I had a couple of male lovers, and I had a couple of female lovers. I don't say I had a great many. I did the Kinsey interview when they were going to do a book on homosexual and bisexual people, the one Kinsey book that I think never got published. It was an eight- or nine-hour interview. Paul Gebhart, who is very good at it, did it. In spite of this, I left a great many things out. There was a lot in it about this borderline between physical and emotional relationships being quite different between men and between women. With men who love men, there is nearly always overt sexual activity. They're designed so neatly and compactly. There are women, I'm sure, who have very intense emotional relationships with other women, which young lesbians today would not regard as sexual relationships.

In fact, if you go back to the turn of the century in popular books for women, there is a great deal of that—all these books by The Duchess and Mrs. L.T. Meade, some of those people whom we don't know much about because it was kind of a disreputable sort of book that they wrote. There was no hint of overt sexuality in any of their women's relationships. Girls in boarding school had crushes on each other, and they wore each other's rings and left messages for each other in the old oak tree. They wrote each other love letters and were jealous of other girls. And they went through school and married nice young men and remained best friends all through their lives, and there was no suggestion of sexuality. Women really sort of had it made in those days. They got away with a very great deal. No one thought.

Queen Victoria's sentiment.

V: Yes. Whatever could they do? In many ways it must have been easier to sustain such a relationship [in those days]. There's that gray area between people being friends and being lovers, and women are not often, even now, suspected of love relationships where men would be.

Well, in Texas I've noticed that any lesbian who wears lipstick and earrings is not recognized at all.

V: We had that in the Midwest until along in the '60s. "Oh, she can't be one—she wears earrings!"

I promise you, you can drive up on a Harley with the biggest butch at your side, wearing boots, a leather jacket, and as long as you've got that lipstick, your heterosexuality is unquestioned. Of course, in Texas there is a breed of woman I call Ranch Women. They wear flannel shirts, no makeup, are butch as can be with a cowboy husband and five kids.

V: Oh, yeah. They do the chores, round up the cattle. It's very hard to tell what's what.

You had affairs with men and then affairs with women, but how did that happen, given that so-called gray area and the climate of the times?

V: I'm not sure. Of course, by the time I had the affairs with women, I had several published lesbian novels, and they made the approaches. These were the femme/butch days, and I was very femme.

Right. But it's long before you've had sexual experience with women, and here you are at the typewriter composing these lesbian novels.

V: Well, you know in general what people do when they go to bed together. You know what you'd like to do, and you know who the people are that you find attractive. In *Whisper Their Love* the girl is seduced by the dean of women in this upper-class junior college that her stepfather sends her to, *but* the dean of women looks like her mother, who had parked her in the country with her aunt when she went out to make a living. So there's that desire for maternal affection. And then the day before her mother's second marriage, she's raped by her prospective stepfather, who was drunk at the time. Which is why I still say—I can't even remember the girl's name now—she was not a lesbian, basically. She was taking refuge from some very traumatic experience in what looked to her like love.

And what would be the difference between someone who was "turned" gay from some traumatic experience and someone who was inherently gay?

V: I don't think we really know what is inherent in this world. We don't know what is instinctual and what is socially bred in people, and I think that some people who turn out to be gay in behavior and life pattern might not be had their experiences been different. I lived in Spain for a year, and I was very interested to learn that while there were a lot of lesbian women, they were mostly upper- and middle-class professional women. And they were not described to one as being lesbian—except that I had an old Irish friend there who knew the whole story of everything and would point them out to me. They were very feminine-looking; Spanish women have a tendency to be—well, in all of the Latin countries femininity is supposed to be a big thing. But there were no advantages for them in being straight.

In Spain in '62 and '63, which is when I was there, women had no legal rights to speak of. Everybody was married; you married young. If your husband wanted to take your children away from you, you'd never see them again. In Portugal at that time, a woman couldn't go on a railway trip without her husband's written consent. So, women who were intelligent and capable of earning a fair income made relationships with other women. It's the Boston Marriage all over again. I understand that in old China, aging, middle-aged widows very often made such relationships. They'd done their duty, they'd had these children, they'd been married and their husband was gone, there was no way that they were going to make a second marriage—so they just teamed up and shared their home. And I'm sure that wasn't all they shared in many, many cases because the Chinese are very realistic about sex. But it wasn't publicly admitted that it was anything but a friendship.

And I can remember when that was quite common among middle-aged and older women in this country. Two nice old widows moving in together, devoted to each other, went everywhere and did everything together. Nobody suspected them. It had its advantages. But nowadays everybody knows everything or thinks they do. And girls feel they have more options—I don't think of the word "girl" as pejorative. Young, single women have more options today, and they may try several of them before they settle on the lifestyle they like. We don't know what is born into people and what is inculcated into them. I don't think that little boys are any more macho than little girls. I think mothers tell their little boys, "Now, don't cry; real men don't cry." And the guy grows up and has ulcers. We have no idea what traits men and women would have if they were just allowed to grow up without these things.

I grew up in a community where a man who loved poetry, much less a man who *wrote* poetry, would be regarded as a sissy. I had a cousin who loved to knit. He learned to knit during an illness when he was a kid, and he knitted beautifully—socks, mittens, all kinds of finger and toey things—but we were not to mention to our schoolmates or anybody that Gilbert liked to knit. Just like we weren't supposed to admit that we played 500, because we were Presbyterians, and Presbyterians didn't play cards in those days. He was a big, tough guy, but he would have been regarded as if there was something wrong with him. Women were supposed to knit, but my mother never mastered the art and was regarded as unfeminine. I've never been able to learn; I end up in tangles. But a man who wrote poetry would have been looked down on—even if his family had lived on the same farm for generations. He was still suspect. Not so much of being "queer," which would have been the word they used, but of being *sissified*.

So, here we are in the 1950s, and you've already written several books.

V: That was right about at the turning point. Then, of course, people who were looking for somebody knew that I should be, within reason, open to persuasion because, after all, I'd written these books. I went to Chicago in the fall of '56, and my first gay book was published at that time.

How did you go from being a PBX operator to a lesbian novelist?

VT: Oh, well I've written always. I can remember at 8 or 9 writing. I remember once my mother got very concerned about my eyesight—until they figured out how nearsighted I am. And she said, in an almost hysterical mood, "I want you to promise me that you'll never write another story!" She thought I was wearing my eyes out. So I said yes, yes. In my childhood, you minded what your mother told you. Of course, I had to write stories, so then I discovered you could write narration in poetry. I read *Evangeline,* and I said, "Hey, what do you know! Here's a story in poetry!" So in order to keep my word, I began writing stories in poetry. Of course, after a while, the whole thing sort of slipped out of my mind, and I went back to writing stories. Children are very creative, you know, until we beat it out of them in one way or another. But we were encouraged to amuse ourselves and keep out from underfoot. We'd read the old mushy romantic novels that our grandmother had been reading for a lifetime, and then we'd act out the story. So getting it down on paper seemed natural.

Do your grandchildren know what kinds of books their grandmother writes?

V: Oh, yes. They read them. I always send each of my kids a copy.

And did your sons, when they were young, know that their mother was a writer of lesbian fiction?

V: Oh, yes. They were very supportive. I don't think they thought very much about it until they got up to, say, junior high school age. Jim, particularly, has been a very supportive person. None of my three kids is gay. That would have been a fine chance for someone to have grown up gay with parental approval, but it didn't work out that way. I think they all probably fooled around with the idea when they were 14 or 15 because that's when boys do those things, and two of them are still bachelors, but they're very woman-oriented.

You worked as an assistant editor at the Regnery Company in Chicago. Did your colleagues know that you were the author of scandalous lesbian novels?

V: Oh, yes. It didn't bother anybody. Charles Lee, the head of the book publishing house, knew about it. He was my boss. The head of the production department, for whom I did some part-time work, was herself a dyke. She never said word one about it, but everybody knew it. The week after I resigned from there, she said, "My partner and I would like you to come to dinner Sunday night." So I met her roommate, whom everybody knew about anyway. They were a pair of really tough, hard-bitten old dykes. I enjoyed them very much; I loved them very much. In fact, it was she who suggested the plot for *Stranger on Lesbos*, and every time that book gets republished, she gets 5% of the take. It hasn't been republished for a while. I gave her a nice, official contract on it. Then on the magazine, the people were mostly not readers, and very few had ever read anything I'd written.

Didn't your coworkers think you might be a lesbian too?

V: I don't think they thought anything special. You see, I was well over 40 by this time, and everybody knows that after 40 you have no sex life. Your libido curls up and dies at about 40—at least for middle-class straight people. This was before Cher was hopping into bed with teenage boys. I'm very amused, by the way. One of those scandalous magazines came out with a frank cover story— Cher's daughter is a lesbian, and Cher was so terribly upset. [The magazine said] "her heart is broken, her life is blighted." And when you consider the life of unabated chastity with which she's conducted herself, you wonder. All of these teenage kids. But they're of the opposite sex—and how opposite it can be sometimes.

I also have a spinal curvature, and many people believe if you're differently abled, you obviously have no sex life! Considering that, some of the sexiest people I know have been very handicapped, some of them in wheelchairs. But it's taken women a long time to learn this too. So I suppose that people thought, *Well, poor thing, it's a nice way to make some extra money,* which it is. I don't make that much though. I make just under a $1000 a year on all my published books together.

Once in a while I've met people who have become upset, but not connected with work situations. When I first came to Tucson 10 years ago I joined the Gray Panthers because they were actively engaged in some good social actions. And one of the women in the Gray Panthers, who is an old, very hard-line Communist, said to me, "They tell me that you write books. What kind of books do you write?" And I said, being the speaker of truth as far as possible, "Oh, lesbian love stories." She recoiled! You're always reading about people recoiling, but I'd never seen anybody do it. She sprang back and said, "But where did you ever find out about anything like that?" And I said, "I took the lab course." We became good friends after that. We're both in Women's International League for Peace and Freedom now, and she's quite a wonderful person, but she was really very upset. She'd never met a dyke before; I didn't look like a dyke. How are we *supposed* to look? Of course, we wear combat boots and dirty blue chambray shirts.

Your characters didn't look like that.

V: My characters, I hope, looked like people. Erika, of course, never had any money to buy clothes. She wore the same coat for years and years. And some of them are very middle-class, like May Sarton's characters. I happen to adore May Sarton; she's my real object of admiration. Her people are all very academic and middle-class. And where you suspect that some of them are gay, you never know. In *Kinds of Love* there's a young, unmarried social worker, and you're never really told that she's a lesbian, but you get the distinct impression that she probably is. This is the way with Sarton's people; they're people, primarily. Some of them are bisexual, like Mrs. Stevens. And of course I think that Sarton herself is basically gay, but certainly she's had some relationships with men.

And your sons were fine with your lesbianism?

V: Yes. I remember when we used to live in a little place called The Colony on the shores of Lake Michigan, in the days when you could still swim in Lake Michigan and not die of cholera or catch your feet in the mud. And we were sitting around the breakwater, and several of the people from the colony were discussing various subjects. My son Jim was there with us. And the question came up, "What is the function of the novel?" Some said it was to forecast the future, and others said it was to portray the present, and finally Jim, who was 15 or so and had been listening, said very soberly, "The function of the novel is to pay the rent." Later, when I found Thomas Hardy saying the same thing in the preface of one of his books, I bought the book for Jim.

You mentioned that business of the emotional/sexual barrier. When you began having affairs with women in the repressive '50s, were you conscious of crossing it?

V: No, I don't think I really felt it to be a barrier. It was the late '50s, and I'd had some sexual experience—obviously; I'd given birth to three children by that time. I knew that my attractions then were very sexual. And, as I say, I was very femme—the other person did the courting.

How did that happen?

V: I don't know. I just happen to attract butch-type women, I guess. I remember a friend of mine saying to a lover who had been unfaithful to her, "And I turned femme for you!"

Describe your butch-femme world.

V: The roles were very carefully laid out. It was an imitation of heterosexual marriage. Some butches demanded that their lover turn over her paycheck; they wanted to handle the money. Straight women now wouldn't put up with that. But it was the only pattern we had. And if you came from a working-class background, usually the man handled the money—though not always. I knew a straight working-class family where the husband turned his paycheck over to his wife, and she doled out his car fare and lunch money. So it depended on where you came from, partly.

Then of course heterosexual love began to change very drastically and very quickly in the late '60s and early '70s, and marriage became very different. Nowadays if you're hetero, you live with somebody for a while, and if you like each well enough, you get married. Even Quakers accept this. Our young people are now often married in their own homes. Some people don't approve, but they recognize it as a pattern. So, suddenly we lost our role models, and we lost our role models sexually too. All these books came out—*The Sexually Adequate Female* by Frank Caprio—telling all the different ways that you could make love and that women could initiate the lovemaking. It used to be that the girl lay there and took it and the husband did all the work, you know.

Everything [in the butch-femme world] was very strictly set up. Somebody would invite you to dinner—"My roommate and I would like you to come to supper Sunday night. Bring your lover." In one case, I knew a woman who had to call and say, "My lover has the flu and can't come, but I'm looking forward to your dinner. What shall I bring?" And the hostess said, "Well, don't come unless you bring somebody; it'll be all couples." Well, heteros don't do that anymore. When you have a party, the guests don't come in like Noah's Ark. Not anymore. And suppose they did? How would you know who to invite with whom? How do you know who's living with somebody, or maybe you have three or four people in open relationships.

So we lost all of our role models over about a ten-year period. We popped out of them in a hurry, somehow. Now straights imitate gays. You know, gays start the fashions. All straight women are having their hair curled, and then lesbians begin to wear long, straight hair, and pretty soon all the straight women are wearing long, straight hair. Gay men wear pink shirts with ruffles, which they did for a while in the late '60s, and pretty soon all the guys in the street are wearing pink shirts with ruffles.

You've described the butch-femme world that you came out into as "carefully laid out." Say a little more about this.

V: When I was first moving in gay circles, moving very slowly in gay circles, in the 1960s in Chicago, I knew several small lesbian clusters. There was the University of Chicago circle and a University of Chicago Press circle, and in a business situation there would be four or six people, and they would all be teamed off—butch-femme, butch-femme, butch-femme. And then usually, if there was any swapping done, you fell out of love with your current person and moved in with somebody else in the same circle. It was like these games where you run around and everybody tries to get a chair, you know. Fruit basket upset. And everybody teamed up differently, and there would be heartbreaks. It was not a real happy situation.

I never, never lived with a lesbian lover—or a male lover, for that matter. I always had my own place, partly because of the kids, and partly because I like living alone. But girls always moved in, and they threw their bank accounts together, and then in six months or six years or whatever, somebody was madly in love with somebody else. Because it would get boring. You know, life was so restricted to such a narrow circle, and you were so secret about it. And then everybody took a new partner, and it was, whose were the records, whose were the books? Who gets the cat?

My friend, Polly, the one who became a femme for the lover who left her, almost went to court to get the dog. I never thought it was an especially appealing dog, but she loved it. And there would be all this anguish, all this heartbreak, attempted suicides—not attempted very seriously, generally. But you'd have these little interwoven groups like a women's sewing circle, and you just associated with those people. And there was really no place to go but the bars. We had *The Ladder*, which was the only lesbian magazine. Look at all of them now!

It took a lot of real true love to stay with anybody under those conditions because you didn't have social sponsorship, you see. If you married a man, you had your picture in the paper, wearing your wedding dress, and the neighbors all knew it. And you had children, which were supposed to cement the marriage. And sure, sometimes they did—otherwise it was tough on the kids. Lesbians went through marriage ceremonies. They exchanged identical rings—the jade band ring was a big thing for us for a long while. You'd see a woman with a jade ring on her wedding finger, and you could be pretty sure she was a dyke. Straight people weren't supposed to know what the ring stood for. And you sent your friends cards on their anniversaries. But it was such a little bitty circle—it's no wonder it didn't work very well. Some of the relationships lasted a very long time. A friend I worked with at the Regnery Company is still in a relationship with her friend. They had their tenth anniversary when I came back from Spain in 1962, so they're going on 40 years. Del Martin and Phyllis Lyon— 40 years or thereabouts together. And they brought up the children of one of them. But they were very open; they were very out. But if you had to keep it a secret—especially if you were a business person or professional, upper middle-class, you had to remain secretive. You didn't make friends with other people very much. It was like living in a harem, except in a harem where the sultans kept changing favorites. And there's always plenty to fight about in any relationship.

If you're sharing your wages, you fight about money. Nearly everybody fights about money anyway. Straight people fight more about money than they do about sex or anything else. Studs and Ida Terkel—well, I know Studs, and Ida was in my Women's International League group, and the subject came up once, How do you manage money? Because Studs would give away his whole royalty check to anybody that needed money. He's that kind of a guy. And Ida was working for a travel agency or something like that. She's a very practical woman. And Ida said, "We split everything right down the middle. My paychecks get split down the middle. Studs' royalty checks get split down the middle." Ida's money came in a steady trickle, and Studs's came in walloping chunks, or sometimes there wouldn't be any for two or three years, but each kept their money separate, almost like two strangers, but they were devoted to each other.

Studs and I had a joke for years. I went on his radio program on WFMT in Chicago, with two guys from Mattachine. They'd send groups out to speak, and these programs would always say, "Be sure to send a lesbian." Well, I was the only lesbian willing to go on radio, much less TV, so I got on quite a lot of these things. I didn't give a damn!

So I went on Studs's program with these two younger guys in 1968-69. And I used the word "screw." I can't remember in exactly what context. And the office boy, more or less, said, "We'll have to blip out 'screw.'" And I said, "I thought I was being nice. What I really meant was 'fuck.'" So it got to be a joke between Studs and me. We'd run into each other, and he'd say, "When are you gonna come on my program and say 'fuck!'"

Tell me about Pearl, the woman you've called "my dearest of all-time lovers."

V: I came back from Spain in 1962, which is when I got acquainted with her. Mattachine was just getting started in Chicago, and she was on its board of directors. That picture above my bed was taken on her 80th birthday. I was 50, and she was 73 when we met. We decided to have an open meeting of Mattachine, and we advertised it in the *Chicago Sun-Times*, which was a liberal newspaper. And they didn't say what I wrote, but they said, "Valerie Taylor, well-known author"—which is a great exaggeration—"will speak." And that was all.

So we sent them 15 bucks, and we took a small ad. They printed it and sent us a tear sheet before they found out what kind of organization Mattachine was. And they sent back our $15 with a note that said, "There are two subjects that are never mentioned in the *Sun-Times*. One is prostitution, and the other is homosexuality." Considering how casually it gets mentioned every place nowadays, it was just incredible how secret everything was! We had the program anyway, and that's where I met Pearl. I knew who she was by reputation, of course, but that was the first time I'd ever laid eyes on her. And she was butch enough to come after me. We had nearly 12 years together, and we never lived together. She was just under 85 when she died. And I think I loved her more than I've ever loved anyone.

A wonderful thing happened at her memorial service. One of the Mattachine guys called me up and said, "I'm going to escort you to Pearl's memorial." I said, "I'm not going. I don't think I could take it." He said, "No, you come. I'll take you out to dinner first." So he took me to this Swedish restaurant, where he stuffed me up with boiled potatoes and Swedish cod fish and one thing and another. You couldn't have grieved if you tried. And we went to this big hall, and there were pictures of her up and around, and they played some tapes. There must have been about 400 people there, including her relatives, none of whom knew I existed. And a whole bunch of boys from Mattachine were there sitting up front. "Boys," I say, because I was in my 60s, and they were mostly in their 20s and early 30s. And when Bill and I came in, those boys turned around and saw us come in and stood up. They knew I was a widow. Her family didn't know it. Nobody else knew it, but they knew it, and they were paying her their homage. This was 1975, the year that I left Chicago. But that has stayed in my mind as the sweetest and most healing thing—to be recognized by my peers, so to speak. Today everybody would know. I had the humiliation of not being allowed at her deathbed as she was dying in the hospital because only "relatives" [were permitted to visit]. Nowadays you get to be the next of kin.

Do fellow Quakers accept you as an out lesbian?

V: It's not an issue. But at one of the Quaker committee meetings of the peace league it was determined that gay issues must not be mentioned at meetings. Our young people might hear something and learn something they shouldn't know. Two middle-aged busi-

nessmen railroaded this through. It was at the end of a committee meeting, and everybody was tired and wanted to get home,
and they just passed it without thinking.

And the woman who was heading that meeting called me and
said, "I think you'd better arrange to meet with these people and
discuss this issue with them." So I did, and I found that they were
very supportive. Some of them didn't even realize what they'd
voted for. And they said, "But of course our young people need
to know." And one of the women of the meeting, certainly a
weighty friend, stood up and said, "Well, our younger son
thought that he was gay and considered committing suicide and
didn't tell us until later. And I wish that we could have come to
the meeting and discussed it intelligently." So they rescinded
what they'd voted on. The Quakers believe that if you pray and
meditate on something, you can be given guidance. But there's a
very practical postscript which says, "But if it doesn't make sense,
don't do it." If it doesn't sound like good, practical common sense,
maybe you want it but God doesn't. Quakerism is a very sensible
kind of religion.

Gay marriages—services of commitment they're called—are also
celebrated. They're announced in the marriage column of our
magazine. Certainly no one would discriminate against you because you were homosexual, but if you spoke of nothing else, then
you would lovingly be told to put another string on your fiddle.

Do you think that the gay liberation movement was such an asset?

V: Over the long run, I think it probably was. People coming up
in their 20s and early 30s now don't realize how things were,
even as late as the 1950s. And I think it's good that they know
what their options are. They don't need to feel guilty. There was
an awful lot of guilt going around in the 1950s and 1960s. And
if you were gay in the 1920s, you were a real outcast. In some
other ways I don't think it is so advantageous that we now have

some liberation. Because there still are a lot of homophobes around. But by and large, if I had a daughter, I'd want her to know what her options were, what her freedoms were, and I would encourage her to choose on the basis of her own wants and needs. None of my three sons happens to be gay. It would have been a great opportunity for somebody to have been a gay kid, but nobody took advantage of it. [*Laughs*] I think you can't have too much information on any subject. We need all the knowledge we can get—in any area. But if you don't think there's a lot of homophobia around, listen to the people who talk about AIDS, assuming that it's all about gay men—"I don't know what you think, but I don't approve of that sort of behavior!" What they mean is not about having AIDS, it's about being gay.

What impact then did the Stonewall era and women's liberation have on you? Did it have any impact?

V: I think it did to a point. I was very pleased when the first books on women's liberation came out, and yet, some of them were not nearly as advanced as I would have liked them to be. And the same with gay liberation. I was very excited, but of course it began with men again, and women were rather slow about coming into it because the penalties for being a lesbian were a lot less than the penalties for being a gay male. We were much more invisible. That's still true to some extent.

But I had mixed feelings about the women's liberation movement. In the first place, NOW didn't want any lesbians in it. "Lesbians will take it over." And actually there's a little element of truth to that: If you've already liberated yourself to the point of being an overt lesbian, it's a lot easier to liberate yourself in other areas. Things like public health care and almost any social issue, things like antiwar activism—if you've thought through some of them, it's easier to think through the rest, and it's easier to come out and be brave and speak up, I think. In other words, [a woman who is] a lesbian has already started to set herself free. And then what's-her-name, *The Feminine Mystique.*

Betty Friedan.

V: And then Betty Friedan came back later and made a statement, you know, years later, about a woman's first obligation is to her home and to her family, but after that she can go out and do whatever. She's a fink, as far as I'm concerned. She's a fink! That Greer woman in Australia was a much better feminist.

Germaine Greer.

V: Yeah. I don't want privileges for women; I want equality—opportunity, equality of jobs. But if we're going to have the rewards of something, we're going to have to take responsibilities also. And to a lot of people who think they're feminists, that doesn't enter into it. They want the same old harem stuff, and then they want everything else along with it. Well, you can't do it. There's too much hard work to be done in the world. I'm sorry to sound mean about it, but when somebody comes up and says, "Well, your first responsibility is to your husband and then your family, and then you can try to put an end to war if you want to." I think it goes together. It all goes together.

Several friends of mine got into women's liberation. They'd bullshit about whether liberated women shaved their legs. Who cares whether they shave their legs or not? Your legs are your legs; I don't care what you want to do with them. Your head is your head; cut your hair any way you want—shave it off, have a Mohawk if you feel like it. I don't care what's on top of their head; I'm concerned with what's inside their head, and what they're doing with it. I don't care if anybody wears a bra or not. Those are trivial issues. What I'm concerned about is, if I get a job, am I going to get the same pay and the same possibilities for promotion that a man is going to get? And am I going to have the right to say what I can do with my own mind and my own body? This is big stuff we're talking about.

And I also don't go along with the women who are very separatist. We had a lot of them in Chicago—the Lavender Lesbians. Oh, God! I stood up on a platform during gay pride week in about '72 or '73, when they were just starting out, and said, "I'd like to remind my lesbian sisters that we have to work with our gay brothers. We don't yet have equality for jobs, equality for housing with straight people here in Chicago." I went twice before the city council to argue this, one dyke with a whole bunch of men, because the other women were afraid of losing their jobs. And they almost hissed me off the platform. Not the straight people, but my lesbian sisters—who I thought were my lesbian sisters. They said, "You will never be welcome in our headquarters again." They couldn't see cooperating with gay men. Now that is plain crazy.

How in the hell do you do anything in the world if you wrench away from everybody who isn't exactly like you? And then we talk about being put upon by straight people. I'm sorry; I'm on a soapbox today. It's very true, you know. You have the one-issue people, and they drag that issue in like a dead rat by the tail, into everything that happens.

Somebody said to me after I'd been working on Quaker committees for a while, "You know, when they put you on a committee, I thought you'd just talk about gay issues all the time, but you never mention it." And I said, "If the issue comes up, I'll mention it." Everybody believes in something, but you don't just limit yourself to that. But a lot of early gay people did. That was all they were concerned about. I can't live that way. You work for something that you believe in, and you also do a lot of other things. Of course, eventually everybody kind of grows up.

People will say *her*story instead of history. People will spell women, w-o-m-y-n. If you want to spell it that way, that's all right.

That's fine. I'm not going to say everybody has to. We have better things to do. If, on the other hand, it's a question of "give this person a promotion" or "let this woman be your electrician or your plumber," that's a different matter. That counts; that's where you're out there making your living. If it's "will you rent your house to these two dykes or won't you?"—that counts. That's reality. I just can't see all this little nit-picky stuff. I've been around too long, and life is too short, I can tell you.

Winn Cottrell
San Francisco, California

Winn Cottrell, 76, lives on the corner of Polk and Eddy streets, in San Francisco's Tenderloin district, a shabby enclave populated by a number of older gay men and lesbians struggling to support themselves on meager Social Security pensions after a lifetime of hard work. Across the street from her building, the Hamilton, a lovingly restored tribute to art deco architecture, sits the Mitchell Brothers' XXX porno theater, the side of which bears a brilliant blue undersea ecology mural featuring whales, seals, and dolphins. Polk Street, at its nicer northern end, cuts through Pacific Heights and dead ends at the bay near the Cannery and Ghirardelli Square. But Winn lives off Polk Street's seamy southern edge, a tightly packed strip also populated by earnest Cambodian immigrants, tattered winos, and desperate teenage hustlers.

Danish modern furniture and clean lines characterize Winn's meticulous apartment, a small studio with a kitchenette and bathroom. Photos and letters of recognition from organizations such as NOW and the Gray Panthers line the wall beside her bed. During our first visit she chain smokes through our conversation and announces several times that she feels disconnected. Our conversation serves as a stimulant, colorful punctuation in an increasingly quiet life. Throughout this first afternoon her disposition is warm and sunny. She serves us cookies and tea.

During visits in 1987 and 1988, however, she is somewhat more confused and drinks more wine at dinner. This makes her maudlin and forgetful. She gives us sloppy parting kisses and cries, and her disorientation is alarming. She takes my girlfriend and me to see Lily Tomlin's The Search for Signs of Intelligent Life in the Universe *at the Curran Theatre, a theater I have not been in since seeing* George M., *starring Joel Grey in the 1960s. We take her to dinner many times. She always tries to give us money, which we decline. She often talks about how sad she is that her daughters aren't closer to her, that they don't really want to know about her life as a lesbian.*

She is "slowing down," as she says, and increasingly absent-minded. An agency known as GLOE [Gay and Lesbian Outreach to Elders] assigns a "friendly visitor" to help Winn out several times a week, cooking and cleaning, banking, paying bills, and answering correspondence.

On one of our last visits she pulls down a raku vase from its resting place atop her letter-lined half wall and pushes it into my arms.

"I want you to take it," Winn says, silencing my protests. "I won't be here forever, and I want you to remember me."

Interviewed May 1986

I Married a 90-Day Wonder

Where are you from?

W: Well, I grew up in the state of Washington, in a little town north of Seattle, right on the Skagit River, or really near. And it was really a wonderful place. There were nice Swedish people, English people, immigrants. And I really liked growing up there.

I'm sure I was a disappointment to my mother because she wanted me to wear little fancy dresses, and that was the farthest thing from my mind. I wanted a pair of jeans, wanted to climb trees and play baseball and tennis and all that. I wasn't able to come up to her expectations about even how to set the table. That was one of my jobs. And so, as a result of all that, I loved her, but I knew there was a separation there that I never could overcome. I don't ever remember her putting her arms around me and telling me that she loved me and everything was OK or anything like that. She really didn't give me very much support, but I guess I got along. That's very important. I don't know that I've ever really gotten over it, but it's been so wonderful for me to be in San Francisco and be accepted, you know? And I accept people, and every place I go I get hugs and "it's so good to see you." So that's meant a lot to me.

I came to San Francisco for the first time before you were born. I was living with this woman, Marcy, and she got a job with the FBI and was transferred to San Francisco, so of course I had to come down too. It was just before the war started, you know, and she was transferred to Washington, D.C., and that was too big a step for me to make, so I went back to Seattle.

In San Francisco at that time there was only one place [for lesbians]. It was Mona's, a lesbian bar, right next to Finocchio's. And a lot of people from across the bay came there too. It was a long time ago; I probably wouldn't recognize anyone who was there at that time. It was really fun. Oh, we used to sing that song, "If you're ever down a well, ring my bell…" You know that song? I hear it every once in a while, still. It was really fun. [*Laughs*]

But in San Francisco now, you know, there's just so much going on. All the groups I belong to—Harvey Milk Democratic Club, Gay and Lesbian Sierrans, San Francisco [Gay and Lesbian] Historical Society. That gives us legitimacy. I'm glad that not everyone is going to bars and running around—the men particularly. I never go to bars anymore. There are so many other places that are so much better to, you know, relate to people. And aren't those [Gay and Lesbian Outreach to Elders] tea dances just the greatest? We've been having 50 or 60 people, and people coming from Palo Alto and San Jose and Marin County. So, we're really doing pretty well.

At what age did you realize that you were a lesbian?

W: Listen, I knew that I was a lesbian when I was 12 years old.

How did you know?

W: Well, because I always wanted to play the daddy when we played house. [*Laughs*] And I was running around the neighborhood kissing all the girls that I could catch. [*Laughs*]

Did anyone think that was strange?

W: Well, I don't know. There were gay people in our town, and my mother was very…well, she ridiculed them.

Tell me about your first girlfriend.

W: It was Marcy, the woman I spoke of. I was college-age, and I remember the first time I kissed her. [*Laughs*] And I said, "Oh, Marcy, I'm so sorry!" And she said, "That's OK, Punk. I wanted you to!" [*Laughs*]

What did she call you?

W: Punk. Punky is what she used to call me. Pun'kin.

And that was that?

W: Well, then we came to San Francisco, and then Marcy went to Washington D.C.; she was transferred there by the FBI, and then she went into the Army because the war was coming and everything. And my brother, who is also gay, had been working in Honolulu for Del Monte, and he came home, and he wanted me to go back to the Islands with him, so dad bought me a little green Chevrolet roadster. We drove it down to San Francisco and put it onto the ship, and we sailed to Honolulu.

In Honolulu, I lived in Fernhurst, which was a "Y" residence. And there were other women there. But no one was really out. I'm sure there were other lesbian women there, but I didn't recognize them.

When the war started, the man that I [eventually] married was in Seattle, and he wanted me to come home. I was really having a good time because there were all these young officers, army officers and everything. I didn't get romantically involved with any of them, but I was having a good time. I worked out in the Navy yard on the labor board. It was a very simple job, interviewing people from Texas and North Carolina. There was a whole influx of people from the United States who came over to work in the Navy yard.

How did you go from Marcy to this fellow who proposed marriage?

W: I had known him. His family had moved to our town when we were both grown up, and he was away at college. Norman was a 90-day wonder. You know, they went to school and got a commission quickly. He was in photo intelligence. So, he came to Honolulu, and there were so many men. I don't know, it was just the pressure, and he was a salesman, and he talked me into it. And I wasn't in love with him, but we were married. Dana, my first daughter, was born in Honolulu, in the Saint Louis School, which was converted into an Army hospital. And I did know a Chinese woman, a lesbian, in Honolulu. In fact, she worked in my office. And when she found out I was going to be married, boy, she was very angry with me, and I guess it was justified. There wasn't a gay community in Honolulu like there is now. Outside of Honey—that's what we called her; I can't remember her real name now—she was the only person that I recognized. She was a little tomboy, and a very good-looking young woman. I thought she was darling, but I was older than she, and there was no point in our [getting together].

So then Norman and I came home and moved to Washington D.C., and all over the country. And Ann, my second daughter, was born in Virginia.

Did your brother, George, think it was strange that you married, given that the two of you knew about each other?

W: Well, the thing is he didn't. Until just recently, just in the last two or three months, he has never really gotten to know me. I've never really been that close to him, but I don't remember his making any remarks. And by that time I was married in Honolulu, he had to go into the army. He was training to be a pilot down in Texas or someplace. We weren't there at the same time.

Did you ever think about women during your marriage?

W: Well, yes I did because Norman turned out to be a—well, not a wife beater—but he used to try to injure me physically without it showing. I never got any black eyes or anything, but he'd put his arms around me and squeeze so hard that I couldn't breathe, and he'd throw me in the shower. Well, after I had Dana, I didn't feel competent. I didn't want to take that much responsibility for both of my daughters, and I didn't know how to support us.

It was very hard to find women in those days, wasn't it? It seems that to have initiated an affair, one would have had to have been very bold.

W: Yes, you wouldn't stop a woman on the streets. I was not that brave. What if you're wrong, or what if they wouldn't admit it? They'd call the police and say this woman is annoying me. And really, I never saw anyone on the street. You just had to come across someone that you could connect with. I don't consider myself bold, really. I know what you mean, though. To make the initial contact, you had to be the aggressor, and you were never sure how it was going to work out. I went all those years without making contact. I had one contact back in Seattle, and it was only when I came to the West Coast that I would see this person, and she was not that interested in me. She had too many other people on the string. So I was isolated. I had to get along with my neighbors, which I did, and we moved so many times. I spent half of my life during that time moving, getting everything settled, getting the curtains up, and then we'd move to some other place. Many of them I didn't like, like Cleveland, but I loved Toronto. I loved Vancouver. And we had good neighbors, friendly people. Even though they weren't gay, I liked them. They were worthwhile people.

So, it wasn't until my older sister was ill with cancer that I drove out. I think I must have had an inkling or a thought that I wasn't going to go back. Because by that time Dana and Ann were young adults. You see, I felt very responsible for them, and to be near when they needed me. I tried very hard to be a good mother. I took them to Europe on bicycles with the Canadian Youth Hostel; we went to seven different countries. We camped across country several times.

Just you and the girls?

W: Yeah. It was really fun. They both live in New York City now. I feel proud. Dana graduated from the University of Toronto, and Ann graduated from Barnard in New York City, and that's where she met her husband, who is a scientist at Columbia. They both married Jewish men.

So, I wanted to visit my sister in Seattle, and I had a Peugeot. My Aunt Joyce, who I inherited this apartment from, tried to dissuade me from taking that trip. She thought it was just terrible to go away and be gone for two months. What would Norman be doing? [*Laughs*] And I'm sure I had the idea that this was the end because both of my daughters were through school and on their own, and they didn't need me anymore. They were adults. So, Dana came with me across country, and I went to see my sister. And Dana went back. And I stayed there till she [my sister] died, and then I came to San Francisco. And I didn't have very much money. And I didn't feel capable. Well, I couldn't get a job that would pay me enough, so I went to work for an older woman on Fillmore Street, and she was neat. Her husband had died after they'd been married only a couple [of years], and they had one daughter. He died in the flu epidemic of 1918. She made no demands on me, and sometimes I used to wonder if she was gay. [*Laughs*] But she wasn't, I guess. I cooked for her, and she was very easy to work for. She had commissary privileges, and so I could buy cheap cigarettes. [*Laughs*] And I always had the weekends off, and I always went off with the Sierra Club. I used to be a hiker. And when I was about 68 I went on a rafting trip down the Stanislaus River and fell in at Death Rock.

What a difference after having lived one way for 30 years, and then you come to San Francisco, and you're hiking, rafting...

W: It wasn't all downhill when I was married. There were a lot of museums where I used to take Dana and Ann when they were little, and Washington D.C. is sort of an interesting city to live in. There were a lot of good things that were free. There were all sorts of good museums and good plays, so, you know, I wasn't suffering all the time. And we had good friends; we played bridge. But I haven't played since. [*Laughs*]

What year was it that you took care of this woman, came out to San Francisco?

W: Let's see? I think I came here in '69. About 20 years ago.

Sixty-nine is a very important year, the year of Stonewall.

W: Well, but you see, I wasn't even aware of it at the time. But let me tell you how I found myself. Do you know Phil [Phyllis Lyon] and Del [Martin]? Well, one day when I was working for the lady I mentioned, I had the television on, and they were on television. Imagine! All that long time ago! And I found out that Phil had an office in Glide Church. Well, I had known about Glide Church, so the next time I had a day off, I just ran down there as fast as I could. And I walked in, and I don't remember anything that I said to her or anything that she said to me, I was just so excited. [*Laughs*] But anyway, I made contact with her. And about three days later—it was just before Christmas—they called and invited me to a Christmas party. Wasn't that wonderful! I saw them just the other day, and I reminded them how they really got me going, helped me find my way.

Now do your children know that you're gay?

W: Yes, I think they know. But they don't seem to want to talk about it. Sometimes when I tried to speak to Dana, she'd say, "Oh, I just don't want to hear about it." And I think they don't feel as close to me as if I were a straight person, as much as I would like to be. I did try to be a good mother, and maybe they don't think I was. I always felt very close [to them]. Because, you know, when they grew up a little bit they were my main contact with the world. And they were both sort of interested in politics, and we used to talk politics a lot, but they don't seem to be that way anymore, and I wanted to be out marching. [*Laughs*] Well, I marched in the demonstrations against the Vietnam War and a whole lot of things because I've become very political, and I want to save the environment and all that.

Do you consider yourself a radical, Winn?

W: Yes. I am a radical. Well, I know that I'm right. [*Laughs*] I had an article that I cut out, and I've lost it. It was a letter to the editor saying why is it that people who are trying to make the world better are always radicals? People who want justice and are trying to take care of people who can't take care of themselves. It was just the nicest little article. I wished that I'd been able to save it because I said, "Yes, that's me!" That writer appreciates all those things that we're trying to accomplish.

Here, let me close that door. The only bad thing in my life right now is there's a colonel who lives across the hall from me, and he's about 85 years old, and we come from the same part of the country, Washington, and he comes from the next county. And we know a lot of the same people from the old days, the politicians and all that. But I was in there one night, and he was trying to get me to go to bed with him. [*Laughs*] And he was telling me about all the prostitutes that he'd brought home. And then he made the remark, "Somebody suggested that you were quite mannish. Are you a lesbian?" And see, I was just laughing at him through all this promotion, and I looked him in the eye and said no. And I hated to do that. There are a lot of gay men in this building, and he always talks about all these "limp wrists" in this building. And one day I said to him, "You know, there's someone in my family who's gay, and he's so much smarter than you are, and he has so much more money than you have, and he's a decent, kindly person, and he doesn't gossip, so I don't want to hear that!" But anyway, he asked me, and I told him no. He used to ask me to come and have a drink with him in the evenings, and he does give me his paper every day, and I used to buy him a bottle of booze to make up for some of it, at least. But really, that was disturbing to me. It really shook me up. So that's why I asked you to close the door—he may be out there eavesdropping. [*Laughs*]

I guess that's the kind of privacy or freedom that a gay elder residential building might afford one—incidents like that wouldn't happen.

W: Well, we've been trying to do that. A group in GLOE tried, and there have been auctions, but women don't have that kind of money. Or if they do, they're not spending it that way.

How are gay elders different? I can hear critics say, "Why do they need their own buildings?"

W: Well, just because you're gay doesn't mean you don't need a roof over your head. I have lived in senior housing at Broadway and Van Ness. It used to be a hospital, but it was converted. But you see, I had all my activities away from that place. And I was young enough then to be able to go out and do things. I didn't have anything in common with those people.

You know, Monika [Kehoe] goes down to the senior center, and she says she just goes to eat. She said she doesn't have much patience for the conversation because all the women there want to talk about is grandchil-

dren, cooking, and their dead husbands. And also they like to talk about their ailments. She says she just likes to eat and then get out of there.

W: I guess it depends upon your personality. My friend Pat used to come to the dances. She was an Army major or something; her shoulders are about that wide. She's a huge woman, and boy, she's got the world by the tail! She tells everyone what to do and how to do it. And she lives at the new senior center and works there and wears her baseball cap. [*Laughs*] And it apparently doesn't bother her, but I just wouldn't like it, although I have a lot of friends my age or near my age through the Gray Panthers. But that's the thing; we're politically together. They accept me, and I certainly accept them because they're bright, and they know how to do things, and they work hard to make things better.

Is there one thing that is important to pass along to the youngest generation of gay people?

W: I think it would be to have confidence in themselves and accept themselves and not to let society try to make them ashamed. And to try and be good citizens. Someday we're going to win this battle, I feel sure. I think a lot of kids commit suicide, and I don't want them to do that.

You were mentioning that you knew you were gay from the time you were 12 and then realizing when you grew up that that wasn't the greatest thing to be.

W: No, that's not exactly it. I knew I'd have a lot of problems. But it was great for me, and I wanted to be who I was, I think, except it was so difficult. That other people didn't understand, that's what I meant.

A friend has told me that her parents said such horrifying things about gay people when she was growing up that she told herself if she turned out to be a lesbian, she'd kill herself.

W: Well, I considered that. I said, "Well, I'll live till I'm 25, and then I'll kick off." But then you get to be 25, and I changed my mind. In spite of everything, my life is the best now that it has ever been.

Lois Hoxie
Berkeley, California

Lois Hoxie was raised in Alameda, Calif., a once-small and sleepy city on the shores of the San Francisco Bay. She remembers playing on the beach with her friends, sitting on the seawall and watching as the tide came in and washed her sandcastles away.

And then the Alameda Naval Air Station was built, and World War II began. Her Japanese-American classmates disappeared, and the beach was no longer hers to play on.

"The world was a much bigger place," says Hoxie, now 62. "I remember the day that Pearl Harbor was bombed, and people were crying, and I can remember asking my mother, 'What's Japan?' There's not an 8-year-old in the world today who would say, 'What's Japan?' They might say, 'Where's Japan?' You know, it was a different world. And then I went to school one day, and all the Japanese kids were gone, and I asked my mother where they were, and she said, 'We're at war with them,' and how baffling that was to me! I wasn't at war with anybody! Especially I wasn't at war with my friends."

Hoxie lives in a small, tidy Craftsman bungalow near the North Oakland/Berkeley border. She is a thoughtful woman, self-effacing, humble, and humorous. She spent years as an administrative assistant but in her early 50s returned to school to become a body worker, practicing acupressure and various forms of massage. She also works with a Bay Area organization known as Namaste, providing emotional support to people living with life-threatening illnesses.

Of her mid-life career change, Hoxie, a Quaker, says: "I feel like I've been pushed off the edge, and I don't even know if I'm flying, but it's a hell of a free fall."

Interviewed November 1986

Catechism, Coming Out, and Me

Tell me about coming out.

L: Well, I feel lucky in a sense because I think I missed the worst of it. I didn't come out until my late 20s. In terms of my sexuality, I realize that I came out of the womb gay, but somebody forgot to tell me what that meant and what that was. I started falling in love at a very, very early age with my little friends and often their mothers and my teachers. I liked older women, you know. But nobody ever said that there was such a thing, so there was no name for it; there was nothing to call it. And you pretended to have crushes on little boys because everybody else had crushes on little boys. But the real truth is, I never had a real crush on a boy in my whole life. Not even once. But I lied about it.

And I went through my teens, I went through my early 20s—talk about being naive or not being totally bright—I fell madly in love with women and still managed not to put a name to it. And I think the most interesting thing is the two women that I fell in love with—they were older women— loved me back absolutely passionately, and they were totally straight. So if anybody wants to make an argument for the right time at the right place, I would have to support that argument because neither of those women had any idea. Well, if they did, they didn't tell me about it. So it was nonphysical—well, nonsexual—nonsexual, absolutely passionate love affairs with women twice my age who were happily married, had children my age. And we used to talk about running away together.

You know, I think back on that now and think, *What?* You know? All right, excuse you, you were 20, 22 or what, but one woman in particular was 44, 45 years old.

And you two talked about running away together?

L: Yeah, yeah. We'd lay down on the bed together and be affectionate. No sexual touching at all. I think back on that, and I think that was absolutely phenomenal that those things can happen, and also that I could stay in this wonderful, comfortable denial place, never acknowledging what was going on. But all of my emotional attraction was for women, usually older, and I loved them absolutely dearly. And you had to pretend to be friends—well, you *were* friends. Because no one ever said there was any other option!

And when I was somewhere around 26 or 27, I moved to San Diego. In fact, I transferred on my job down to San Diego, and I lived down there for two or three years, and that's where I came out. Somebody put a name to it. Although I had left home at 17 and had lived very independently away from family and parents and stuff like that, San Diego was a long way from home, and I met a young woman there. She was about my age when I met her, maybe just a little bit younger. She was a secretary, and I worked for the Navy at the Naval Training Center. Right away, instantly, we got to be friends.

We used to sit around in my apartment and talk, and I realize now she was a lesbian, but I didn't know it. And she knew I was a lesbian, but I didn't know it. And so she'd sit there, and she'd direct the conversation and say all these things, and they just floated right over my head. Right over my head! I wish I'd taped them. I wish I could go back and listen to them now, and I'm sure I'd say, "Oh, my God, Lois! How could you have missed it?" I truly didn't know.

What did she look like? Just like any other young, American woman?

L: Oh, yes! Very definitely. There was nothing stereotypical about her at all. This was in the early 1960s, so most women were still wearing makeup. We hadn't gotten so far as to say, "I'm wearing jeans and a sweatshirt, no matter where I go and what I do, and if you don't like it, shove it!" We weren't quite there yet. People blended. She blended. She was quite an attractive young woman. Wore heels and hose to work. Hell, we all did, when I think back on it now! [*Laughs*] Strikes me as almost funny. I haven't had a skirt on for probably better than 20 years. But this was before that.

But later, when we talked about those conversations, she told me how frustrated and angry, furious, she was because she thought I was just not cooperating or not willing to come out of the closet. And that is sort of interesting. Thinking back on those evenings of conversation, how frightened we must have all been that we couldn't even talk about ourselves. Or at least that was her perception. I was just not bright enough to know what was going on. But there were two women sitting, and the reality was, in all likelihood, that they could not even come out to one another because the environment was so terrifying. That is sort of interesting to think back on.

How did you make that leap and come out?

L: Well, Carol and I became very good friends, and she finally just gave up on me, as she worded it later. We were sitting in my living room one day—I was sitting on the sofa, she was sitting over on the chair—and she said, "Of course you know that I'm a lesbian." And I said, "Oh, really? Are you?" And the truth of it was I wanted to jump out the window. I was terrified! But I was Joe Cool. I said, "Oh, uh-huh. What'ya know about that? Want another Coke?" I was terrified. Now, here I was, as latent a lesbian as you could possibly be, but terrified when somebody else—a dear friend—said that *she* was a lesbian. I don't know what that's all about, but I remember clearly the feelings. And I guess I said, "That's nice." And still nothing much happened for me.

And I can't tell you how long a period of time went by, but the way I came out was standing in my bathroom. I was standing in my bathroom, in an apartment in San Diego, brushing my teeth. And you've seen the electric lightbulb in the cartoon strips that comes on over somebody's head, and that is actually the way I came out—brushing my teeth one morning I said, "Oh, my God! [*Slaps her forehead*] That's it!" And my whole life made sense.

What made sense to you?

L: I was a lesbian. That explained all of the attractions from the time I could remember, from the time I was a little kid. It all made sense. And it was a wonderful feeling. And you see, whereas somebody had forgotten to tell me there was such a thing, they also forgot to program me to feel any shame or any fear because I've talked to other people whom that acknowledgment depressed, you know, made them want to commit suicide. I felt terrific. I felt absolutely great! I never thought about the outside world or what the ramifications might be. It was just a settling of something about me. That *Well, of course, that's what it is! All these women that I've loved—good Lord, there's a name for it! That's what it is!* I felt absolutely elated! And then I said [to myself], *What are you gonna do about it?* Hmm. So I said to myself, *Are you unhappy with your life?* I said no. *Are you content the way things are?* I said yeah. *Well then, it would probably be very foolish to go out and make any great, huge changes in your life.*

So, I decided not to make any changes in my life at all, but I was terribly pleased that I had a name for the things that I was feeling. And if memory serves me right, an entire year went by of my living exactly the same life and one day wanting to know how the other half lived, what it was like to meet more people like myself. By then Carol was going with somebody as a couple, and she lived a little distance away—not too far. And I remember calling her on the phone one night and saying, "I'm ready. I want to go to a bar." In those days there was nowhere else to go, of course.

And whenever the next Saturday night was, why, that was my first trip to the gay bars in San Diego. And I remember what that was like. I remember my own cultural shock. Because I wasn't prepared for many of the things I saw there. In those days men couldn't dance together; women could. It was like Halloween—seeing men in drag.

So it was a mixed bar?

L: Yeah. The bar that I preferred going to was a mixed bar.

In fact, the all-women bars I didn't care for.

What turned you off about those?

L: They were tough! I remember one bar—I don't know that I remember the name of it—but it was tough. A tough crowd of dykes. I don't think we were using the word positively in those days.

What did they look like?

L: As I recall, everyone of them had a cue stick! [*Laughs*] That's what it seemed like, you know. I suppose they looked like we all look today. More of the stereotypical butch, beer-drinking crowd. Fights. Sort of scary for me, you know. And I didn't enjoy it. I also enjoyed gay men tremendously. And still do. In fact, they were the ones who helped me and took me under their wing and escorted me into this very strange world. And they were my best friends. I was scared of women. See, I wasn't scared of women till I found out I was gay. Then I was scared of women. [*Laughs*] So, it was the fellas who took care of me, so I very much preferred a mixed bar.

What were you afraid of?

L: All of a sudden, I guess, I didn't know how to act anymore around women. I thought, *Well, uh, gee whiz, everybody wants somebody. How do you ever find a partner?* Again, there was nowhere to go but bars. That means that obviously what needs to happen is one night you are sitting at the bar having a beer, and you look up, and "their eyes met and they knew." I mean, how else is this gonna happen, you know?

It occurred to me that I had to make choices. The world was very much divided into butch and femme, so obviously you had to make some decision here as to what role you had to play. It never occurred to me that things should evolve naturally. I must have decided on a butch role because I had some awfully smart little boots, as I recall. [*Laughs*] And I guess I was back up here in the Bay Area because nothing really extraordinary happened in San Diego at all. I was much too shy to ever approach somebody. I had no idea how to do it. There was nothing in my culture, nothing in my society that teaches a woman how to approach another woman. So I sat on a barstool and nursed a couple of beers, talked to the fellas, and watched the women.

And once you decided you were going to be a butch?

L: Didn't do a thing for my shyness or my personality. That didn't help me any.

Were there clothes that you had to abandon or adopt?

L: No, I don't remember really having to abandon any because I think I had pretty tailored tastes to start with. [*Laughs*] I was just never the pink-blouse type, I'm afraid. It was just you spiffed up a bit more when it was time to go out. By the way, before I leave San Diego I should probably say there were some incidents down there. Especially in the downtown area. We did park several blocks away [from bars]. And San Diego is and was at that time very reliant upon the defense industry for its economy. So, I had lesbian friends who worked in the defense industry and had stickers on their cars. And I worked on a military base and had stickers on my car to get onto the military base, and we parked some distance away so our cars could not be identified. And I do remember times when the light [in the bar] would flash on and off, which meant the vice squad had just walked in. And in the event that you should be doing anything in the back room, stop doing it.

There was a front room and a back room?

L: Yeah. The bar that I mostly hung out in was called the Barbary, and it was in Ocean Beach in San Diego. And what there was was a front part that was a bar, and then there was a dance room in the back. It wasn't so much that it was two rooms, but it felt like two rooms. And the signals that they had—like if guys were dancing together. Something like that. Or, as I say, if anyone was doing anything they shouldn't, why, they would either flash the lights or plug and unplug the jukebox. So there'd be some signal. And I very clearly remember that. And I remember people losing their jobs. But I cannot honestly say that I recollect any personal fear.

Did you read about people losing their jobs?

L: No, I knew people personally who lost their jobs. I knew some women in San Diego at that time who had been dishonorably discharged from the Marine Corps, and I can sure remember their horror stories around the witch-hunts that took place in the military. But I never experienced any personal fear or discomfort around it. I really can't say that I did. Nor have I really to this day. So, either I've led a charmed life, or I'm just not smart enough to be scared when I should be. [*Laughs*]

Anyway, moving back up here, I was now this newly emerged lesbian, and I was coming home. I was coming home to towns that I knew, to parents, friends, relatives. To all this incredible familiarity, except I was a different person now. And I did not have the foggiest idea of where to go for contact. Although I understand that there are some very bold people—mostly men—who could ask a taxi cab driver where a gay bar was, I certainly couldn't do that.

And after I was up here for a few weeks, my furniture still hadn't arrived yet, so I was staying temporarily with my folks. I got a phone call one night. One of my gay male friends had come up right behind me practically and was looking for a job. I ended up getting my own apartment, and Don stayed with me for a period of time until he got on his feet. And we used to go out together at night, and we would hop in his car and drive up and down the streets, peering into the bars as if one of them was going to flash some magic sign.

And one night we went over to Sausalito 'cause we'd heard that we'd surely find something in Sausalito. Neither of us really had the nerve to go up and ask anybody. And there was a bar called the Bridgeway at that time. And Don and I wandered the streets and went in this bar and that bar, just stuck our heads in. You didn't even need to have a drink; you just stuck your head in and knew. And we got to the Bridgeway, and we opened the door and stepped inside, and Don looked at me, and I looked at him, and we said, "O-o-oh, we're home." It was a terrific mixed bar at the time. So once you locate a bar, you're home free, right, because you're going to find out where they all are.

Well, Don wasn't all that crazy about women, and he didn't like mixed bars, and he really wanted to go where the fellas were. So, for a long time, I drove every Friday night and Saturday night from Oakland to Sausalito because it was the only place I knew of. And I often wondered what the neighbors thought. Here Don and I were living together, and we would go out on a Saturday night, both of us all spiffed up, and he would get in his car, and I would get in my car and we'd say, "Good night, see you later!" [*Laughs*] It must have looked peculiar, if anybody had paid attention to that.

Anyway, my history was still sitting on the barstool. I never did approach anybody. Well, once I did. Once I went up to this woman, and I asked her if she would meet me for brunch. I guess it was at Romeo's or something like that—a brunch spot in the Haight-Ashbury. And she said, "Yeah, sure." And so I showed up a few minutes early. I think it was the next day. And she didn't come, and she didn't come. And about an hour or two later, she came in with this whole great group of people, and they went over, and they sat down somewhere together at a table, and that's as far as that date went.

And I'd hear people say the strangest things. I was totally naive. I'd had no sexual experience at all. I remember sitting in the bar and hearing the woman next to me say to another woman, "Well, she may think she's butch, but I kissed her, and believe me—she ain't no butch!" And I thought, "My God, you've even got to kiss a certain way!" [*Laughs*] This was, "Oh, my word, there's all this code that I don't know anything about at all!" You know, it was very scary business. So, that was my early coming out experience. Bars is all there were. And basically, I sat there and watched the world go by every Friday and Saturday night. [*Laughs*]

And what changed your luck?

L: Funny. Now, that doesn't mean I didn't fall in love. I would fall in love with these people, and we would always end up to be very good friends, and I always listened to them while they told me about the people they were madly in love with. You know, that role. I was the best friend they ever had. What broke that was, of all the unlikely places, my workplace. There was a woman there; we were fairly good friends. She was married, happily. Had a daughter and definitely drank too much, and occasionally a group of us from work would go out.

I didn't join them very often because I'm not much of a drinker. All of those nights in the bar, you know, I could get a couple of beers to last me a long time. And this crowd really drank quite a bit, so stopping after work for a drink normally turned into an all night thing where everybody was bombed by 11 o'clock and nobody had had dinner. That wasn't a lot of fun for me, so I didn't do that with them very much. But there was this one night when a group of us went out, and we ended up over at one of the women's houses. And this woman from work,

Dolores, came up to me and said something like, "I have got to talk to you." OK, I'm always available for someone to talk to. "Well, not here," she said. OK. So we ended up going down to another bar. And I've forgotten the exact order in which she said things, but she informed me that she knew all about me. She knew that I was "one," and she thought maybe she was too. And that she was really very attracted to me, and she wanted to have some sort of a relationship. And that scared the hell out of me!

Number one, as far as I was concerned, she was straight. She was married. She had a daughter, and I was not remotely attracted. I mean, she was a nice person. And I spent several months saying, "Dolores, for heaven's sake, go back to your husband. You're crazy! I mean, you're nuts. I don't want to have anything to do with this!" And I was pursued. I'd never been pursued before. I'd always done the pursuing and to absolutely no avail whatsoever. And now, all of a sudden, someone was pursuing me, and I wasn't interested. Ain't that a bummer?

She would come and knock on the door, middle of the night, and this was sort of a night and day bombardment. And at some point I sat her down and told her exactly the way I felt. I said, "I don't love you. I think you are a really nice person, and I don't love you." And I was totally honest and said, "If you still want me to live with you, I will, as long as you know what the truth of it is—this is my free trip, that for the first time in my life, somebody loves me." And she agreed to that.

Now, geez, these are times when everybody was closeted, so you can't imagine how this shook up families and the workplace because she and her husband, Wally, had been considered such an ideal couple. And Dolores left her daughter with her husband. That wasn't done much in those days either.

What did she tell her husband?

L: I think she told him the truth, and I think he was the only one she told the truth to. And what she said to other people I don't know exactly, except that she was bored. "Yes, Wally's a nice guy, and I'm bored to death." She was under incredible pressure from drinking friends, bowling friends. Couples that did things together—their social life was one another—couldn't understand that, didn't like it. And her mother would call up and say, "He beats you?" "No, he doesn't beat me." "He's mean to your daughter?" "No, he's not mean." "He doesn't provide?" "Yes, he provides." So the family is, [*incredulous tone*] "Why are you leaving? He *bores* you?" So, you can't share fully. Again, not even with your family!

Wally *was* pretty dull. I mean, I always pictured Wally sitting in a chair reading a newspaper. Not a whole lot more. But you don't break up a family for this. So again, when I think of the constriction of those times—there really wasn't anyone you could share that with, and it doesn't make any sense. Just doesn't make any sense that you move in with a girlfriend.

And we worked together, and needless to say, I came to love her very much. Didn't take all that long. And we had really a very good life. She was alcoholic, and that was the flaw in our relationship. Every once in a while she would suddenly come out from wherever she was—the living room, bedroom, dining room—and she would say, "I've got to leave you, you know. I want to be here, and I want to spend the rest of my life with you, but I've got to leave you." The first four years we were together I lived with that. It was almost more than I could stand. And I think it was simply that the social pressure was so great to go back to Wally, from her friends, from her family. We didn't have support as a gay couple. You know, a couple fellas you run around with, a couple women you run around with, but that greater world out there was pushing at her to go back. That was like acid dripping in my stomach, and I never knew when that was going to happen. And there was all the fear and all the agony of her coming out and saying that, just even saying it.

Then she started sort of seeing him again, sort of dating him

again. That was very, very agonizing for me. And one day it finally reached a climax when she said it again, and she was still seeing him and talking about leaving. And something snapped in me
at some point, and I said, "I'll help you pack." Because I could not
stand to live that way. It got to the point where—you know a situation where you dread or fear something happening so much
that it would be a relief to have it happen because it's worse living with the anticipation of it? That's exactly what happened to
me, and so I assisted her. And she went back to him, and I was
absolutely devastated.

And there again, here we were both in the same office at work,
me in tears, me trying to pretend I wasn't crying, people not
knowing why. Nobody you could share with; nobody you could
talk to about it. Actually, people feeling more celebratory of the
fact that Dolores and her husband were back together. Those
were really agonizing times. My mother was still alive at the time;
she was in a convalescent hospital. I wasn't out to my parents; not
many people were out then. But I remember going to see my
mother one time and her wanting to know what was wrong. And
I said, "Well, Dolores has gone back to her husband."

And I've so often thought about my mother's comment because it seems to me that most people in our culture would be
pleased when a married couple gets back together. Four years
they'd been separated. And here's this lovely daughter, and you
just expect people to say "isn't that lovely?" You know, a happy
ending. And I said to my mother, "Dolores has gone back to her
husband." And my mother said, "There, there, now dear. A lot of
water's gone under that bridge." Whatever that meant. But that
was part of her wisdom—"a lot of water's gone under that bridge;
don't you worry, she'll be back." And I thought later, *Wow, all the
times we think we're being so cleaver by being closeted.* And I don't
say my mother consciously knew, but on some level, you know,
people know—back here somewhere [*places her hand on the back of
her head*].

*During those four years did your parents ever ask you, "Lois, when are
you going to get married?"*

L: My parents never did that to me. Again, I think that is a unique
experience from people that I talk to. My mother never did. My
mother probably would have been a lesbian if she'd had the
chance. I wouldn't be at all surprised, thinking back. My mother
was far more likely to say, "Plenty of time, plenty of time. Don't
rush into anything; you got plenty of time."

But what happened with Dolores going back to her husband—
she was gone two weeks. Two weeks. And I moved, you know,
couldn't afford the apartment and had taken a smaller apartment
somewhere. We moved back in together, and that was the last I
ever heard about her leaving or going anywhere. So I have to assume that was something that she had to do. That she had to try
one more time. Because when she came back, the next couple or
three years were probably the best that we ever had. She pretty
much gave up drinking. I'm not even sure how that came about.
And we lived a really quality life.

Dolores died of cancer at the age of 44, after a 15-month illness. And that's sort of interesting too because no one ever questioned that I was the primary person. Really some strange things
for that time—I'm now up to 1972. And no one ever questioned—
not the hospital, not the doctor. Her husband did not interfere,
whatever our decisions were. Nor did her daughter. Her family
would come out to visit from Minnesota. Her mother had died,
but her father came out. A couple of sisters came out, a brother
came out, and all of them were so supportive of me. It's as if
everyone knew, and I don't think they did. They saw a love relationship. What I remember her family saying when they came out
is, "Lois, you can't imagine how relieved we are that Dolores has
somebody like you." Other people haven't had that experience. So
I had the support of her family; I had the support of my own
family.

When Dolores died—she was very popular at work—I was treated like the widow or the widower. We worked in that same place all that time, and we were not out to anyone.

Would people at work ever ask you if you were seeing anyone, what you did on Saturday night?

L: No, I don't remember that ever being a problem. But I've always told people what I was doing, and in that respect I've always been out. You know, I'd say, "Dolores and I are going to a show," or something like that.

What I was still doing—I gave it up shortly thereafter—I was still taking the token gay man to the office party. Boy, did I stop that. But anyway, at that time I was still doing that kind of thing. But when Dolores died, the people who offered me condolences —it was just totally different than two friends living together.

God, I remember this woman coming up to me [*Laughs*]—and we weren't close at all, she was kind of strange, she was a party animal—she came up to me one day at work after Dolores died, and she said, "Oh, I remember how I felt when my husband died." She said, "It was four months after he died that I could even da, da, da." Whatever those stories were. And I suddenly realized that people were relating to me as if I'd lost a spouse, which I had. But we weren't out, and I really believe that most of them did not know. They were responding in this very, very caring way without putting a name on it.

My two theories—the people you think you absolutely have aced, that they don't know a thing, they're the ones who always know. The ones you've been so obvious around, that couldn't *not* know, they're the ones who have no idea. People always seem to fall into those two categories. So, that experience with Dolores is, first of all, what broke me out of sitting on the barstool, watching the world go by, and also gave me some really interesting experiences around still being closeted yet still being pretty much myself and receiving support and caring from people who probably really didn't know what was going on.

That was sort of a catalytic event in my life because it was shortly after that I came out of the closet. I really came bursting out of the closet, and part of it was anger. Part of it was saying, "I don't ever want to go through that again alone. I don't ever want to go through that again without community support, without any acknowledgment. You know, that isn't OK with me anymore. I want my share. I want what every straight person gets."

How did you come out of the closet "in a big way" after that?

L: Well, a couple of years went by, and then I found a true love. 1974. And this is a woman, Sharon, that I lived with for ten years that was probably the most perfect love that I've ever had and maybe ever will. And during those ten years together, we just— maybe it was the atmosphere, maybe it was the climate, things were beginning to change.

How did I come out in a big way? I had converted to Catholicism when I was in my early 20, and I played that little game until I came out. At the time I came out, I simply stopped going to church. I didn't have any big trauma about it. I even felt OK about the church. It's just that I figured they didn't go together. Somehow, if I was going to live a gay lifestyle, I couldn't go to church. So, OK, I wouldn't go to church. It was no big deal.

So, I had been away from the church for a while, and different things happened to me. I started going to MCC. Have you heard of them in your travels?

Yes.

L: OK. I hated 'em myself. I thought, "Evangelical—oh, my." But it was something other than the bar, OK, so there was a place where you could meet three or four other gay people. It was a pretty small congregation. [*Laughs*] But the foundation of that church tended to be very fundamental, and so they tended to lean in that direction, which has never done very much for me.

And I came home from work one day, and I lived on a cul-de-sac, and there was a car parked there, and there's never a car parked there. And I looked, and I said, "Geez, it looks like the priest from Saint Pascal's. I don't know what he'd be doing down the cul-de-sac."

And I got out of my car, and I started in the house, and he looked at me, and I looked at him, and he said, "Hello, I'm Father Ericsson." He said, "Are you Catholic?" And I said, "Yeah." And he said, "But I don't see you at Saint Pascal's?" He was an interesting guy, and back in those days he was just calling on the neighborhood. People haven't done that for years. It's like getting a doctor to make a house call. He said, "I haven't seen you in the parish?" I said, "No, I don't go to church." And he said, "Well, why don't you go to church?" And I said, "Have you got a minute, Father?" He wanted to know why I don't go to church? I'll tell him why I don't go to church! [*Laughs*] And I invited him into the house, where I proceeded to say, "I don't feel welcome at Saint Pascal's. "Why is that?" he said. "Because I'm gay," I said. "Yes, but," he said, "why don't you feel welcome at Saint Pascal's?" Maybe he didn't hear me. I said, "Because I'm gay." And he said, "Yes, but at Pascal's you don't feel welcome?" OK, watch my lips, "I am a *homosexual!*" And still again, there was this totally puzzled look on his face. "Yeah, well, so OK, you told me that." And *here* was a brand new experience. Here stood this young priest saying, "What's that got to do with anything?" Here's a young priest standing there saying, "I don't happen to think that's a sin." Well, we became great friends. I went back to church. Sharon decided to come with me. My best friends were made up of an elderly monsignor, Brian Joyce, who was the chancellor of the diocese and was in residence at Saint Pascal's, the associate pastor Jim Ericsson, and a rather large handful of assorted nuns who were attached to the parish school. And Sharon and I developed the nun-a-month club, where we would have one of the nuns over for dinner so that they could get to know us, and they would get to smoke. Because they wouldn't even smoke around each other or anybody else.

We became family. We were very close to them. And we were out to them totally.

And a lot of that came about because of Old Saint Mary's, downtown Oakland. The different parishes used to adopt it for a Sunday. They would sponsor, go down there, and take all the food and feed the elderly and the poor, the disenfranchised people. And I got this brilliant idea. I wondered what would happen if I got a bunch of volunteers from MCC to go down and join Saint Pascal's and help out over at Old Saint Mary's and have all those strange folk meet one another over the kitchen sink? And so that's exactly what happened, and it was just a crazy, wonderful Sunday. All those straight parishioners and all those nuns and all those priests and all those little faggots in there, chopping onions and carrots and running around, picking up people and being willing to do the crappy jobs, taking out the garbage and doing the dishes and all that sort of thing. And they got to talking to one another. An outcome of all those people getting to know each other was that Margot, our very favorite nun, went down into the basement of the convent and found an old crucifix, an altar cloth, and some other religious articles that she brought to MCC and donated to them.

And of course these nuns were cleverly disguised as normal people—they weren't wearing habits, right? And the shock of so many of the gay men and lesbians there saying, "You're a who? You mean a *nun* would come down here to our services and bring us this stuff and sit through this service?" It was just a very wonderful time. People got together and had this kind of exchange.

In 1976 the Catholic church—they did what they call a town hall sort of a thing, for maybe the only time in history. The bishops actually asked for feedback from us common folk about what we really thought about things. And they had some categories already selected—peace and social justice–type things. And there'd be a panel to hear you. And I spoke at some point about gay and lesbian people. So that kind of coming out—serving on committees within my parish, being obviously an open couple. We were receiving communion. This was a very unique parish. So there was a coming out process already taking place. And then in 1978 Proposition 6 appeared on the California ballot.

The Briggs Initiative.

L: The Briggs Initiative. We had many school teacher friends, and we decided since they really could not work on this initiative—except at great personal risk—we needed to do so. And we went over to San Francisco one day to hear Harvey Milk speak to Dignity.

The gay Catholic group?

L: The gay Catholic group. And Harvey made a plea for coming out of the closet, that this was the only way to freedom. And he said, "Go home and take out your Christmas card list, and write a letter to everybody on your list, and come out." And of course, we were also doing a great deal of educating around gay issues. We were talking about child molestation and all of the myths and all of the fears and the garbage. School teachers taking your child off to the rest room or whatever they were supposed to be doing. So there was this tremendous educational thing going on too.

Sharon and I were so moved by Harvey that we did exactly that. We came home, and we took out our Christmas card list— which was very large—and we wrote a letter, and we came out of the closet to every friend and relative we had in the state of California, plus a few that weren't in the state. Everybody! And I'm talking about 100 or 200 people probably. And we enclosed literature with our letter. So that was a major coming out.

What was the result of that?

L: It was very positive. Again, I don't know whether I've led a charmed life or what. There was not one negative reaction. It's not that everybody wrote back, but there were a few people who did write back, and it was positive. Absolutely positive. There was no bad experience that came out of that. Not one.

Then we heard someone from the *Oakland Tribune* wanted to interview gay couples for a series on gay couples who had been together longer than six weeks. Ann Bancroft was the reporter. And somehow I got in touch with her, and she called and she said, "What's your story?" Sharon and I had been together for four years by that time, 1978. We were very active in Saint Pascal's, and we were an open lesbian couple. Well, that must have struck her fancy, since there weren't a whole lot of openly gay couples running around the local Catholic churches.

She came out with a photographer, and that made Sharon considerably more nervous than it did me because of her parents. Sharon's parents lived here in Castro Valley, and they were a very close couple. Yes, they knew. Of course they knew; they were among the first to know. But they were uncomfortable with it.

Anyway, Ann Bancroft came out—sounds like the movie star— and she did an interview with us, and she said, "I don't know if or when this will ever be published." This was in July of '78, and we said OK, fine. And we were not contacted again, and we actually came to forget about it.

One Saturday morning in October we got a phone call. Somewhere in town the newspaper had hit the street, and somebody said, "Oh, my God, you are all over the Sunday *Tribune!*" So many months had gone by, and at the time it had sounded like great fun. "Oh, yeah sure, we'll do it!" [*Laughs*] And then we hit the paper, and it was scary. The Sunday *Tribune* is thick. There's the first section there, which tells you who you're at war with today. [*Laughs*] And in the very next section, there we were. On that front page. Picture! The whole thing. I mean, boy, you couldn't have missed it! It was just a huge article. We took up maybe a third of the page. The reporter had ended up doing four couples, but we led with Sunday.

They were doing it in installments?

L: Yeah. And they did one on Monday, Tuesday, and Wednesday. Well, who reads Monday, Tuesday, Wednesday? We were the big lead off. O-o-oh. And it was a pretty good article. There were a couple things that she said that we don't feel we said, or certainly we didn't mean that. Poetic license. She said we wanted to be recognized as a married couple. I don't think we exactly said that, although we probably would today, so it doesn't make any difference. For the most part, it was a positive article.

Now, I can't say that there was nothing negative that came out of that. But very little, very little. We were scared to death. We were absolutely scared. We hadn't given any thought to what doing that might really be like. We really hadn't. We hadn't thought about the circulation of the Sunday *Oakland Tribune.* And it occurred to us afterward that there are crazy people out there. I remember we went somewhere during the day—and we lived on this cul-de-sac—and we turned that corner onto the street, and neither of us said anything to one another at that time, but we shared later that there was fear. We felt some fear. People burn crosses, you know. There are some nutty people out there. Here we had come out in a major newspaper. A huge article with our pictures! [We were] listed in the phone book.

Well, we got some phone calls. Two or three phone calls. We got a phone call from a couple in Modesto who were thrilled and delighted and asked if they could come to church with us one day.

I got a call from a little old lady, an elderly lady, and she said, "Hello, dear, you don't know me. My name is so-and-so, and I'm a straight woman, and I just wanted to tell you girls how wonderful I think it is that you've done this and just keep up the good work!" That kind of thing happened. Instead of getting hate mail, I got letters from strangers. Got letters from people saying thank you, which is an incredibly moving thing. People who, for their own reason, can't do it, can't come out. But what we talked a lot about in that article was our experience at Saint Pascal's. Now *there* some negative things started happening.

If you know anything about the average Catholic parish, they got a 5 o'clock mass on Saturday night, and they got one at 7 and one at 9 o'clock on Sunday, and probably one at 10:30, and then there's the noon mass. Because they're going to get you. What I forgot was that each one of those masses tends to almost be an individual parish. People tend to go to the same mass. Whatever their lifestyle is, they tend to go to the same mass.

So, Sharon and I would go to the 10:30, and I was on the liturgy committee. She was active with the chorus, but those were mostly the 10:30 people. But we sort of made a mistake along the way by saying "Saint Pascal's." We were friends with all the nuns, with all the priests, you know, with the monsignor, and with the very active, lively group of liberals that went to the 10:30. We forgot about all the other folks.

So, here comes some Saint Pascal parishioners who are picking up their Sunday papers and are saying, "What? First of all, we want to know what priest told you it wasn't a sin because that's not what my Baltimore Catechism said! And they're receiving communion every Sunday!" Some of them just went bonkers. They really went bonkers!

It happened at a very bad time. It happened when the old monsignor had retired, and we didn't have a pastor. We had a young pastor who wanted to be a full pastor when he grew up and, therefore, didn't particularly want to go out and slay dragons.

Wanted keep a much softer profile than that. We had parishioners who were taking up petitions to the bishop—to do what with us we're not real sure. Whether we were going to be crucified or just denied communion, I don't know. But some unpleasant stuff came out of that.

The people who had supported us always supported us. We didn't lose our support group. We didn't lose it because we'd gone in honest. We went in as an openly gay couple. Well, those people aren't going to abandon you. But, now you had some other people coming in, and some of them were "influential"—that usually means they're contributing bucks when the plate goes by. We shared the same building and the same grounds, but we weren't really all that aware of each other. So that was a real lesson. And that became difficult, and it became painful, and things changed a lot for us.

The church had changed. A lot of the nuns and priests had left. There'd been a changeover; that's going to happen. And shortly after that we moved to Hayward. I mean, we hung in for that. Things were never resolved to our satisfaction. We wanted to talk to the people bringing the charges, and this young priest was trying to keep it separated. And we were saying, "No, we think we should confront this. There's no reason why we can't sit and talk." And he didn't want that to happen. He dropped by the house one day, and during the course of conversation he said he would certainly hope, considering all the pain and agony it had caused everybody, that if we had it to do over again that we wouldn't do it. And I said to him that I didn't think that would be the case; I think that I would still do it again.

Suggesting that you and Sharon were the source of all the trouble.

L: Yeah. And you know, he's a sweetheart of a guy, and he struggled so with that. He was horrified that we would go do the same thing even though there was a cost.

We moved to Hayward, and I was rapidly out of my whole church, Catholic, Christian [orientation]. And I'm not sure I ever was [a "real" Catholic], but for a lot of years it provided me with an atmosphere in which to do my spiritual stuff. I don't think I left the Catholic church as much for theological reasons because I don't think I had ever really been that involved in their theology, as funny as that may sound.

We had some wonderful years there, and I'm very glad that we were there, and I'm very glad that we made so many friends, and we sent those people off into different parts of the country with whole new ideas about people. There are a lot of people who feel differently about gay and lesbian issues because we were in their lives, and I'm happy about that.

But to continue it, to continue that battle, it's just too exhausting, which is how we stumbled into Quakerism. We found that we were aligned not only socially and politically but theologically. You know, if you're going to sit in a silent meeting for an hour, you know, you don't have to deal with anyone else's theology. You don't have to deal with any sexist language because there isn't any language at all. You don't have to fight through anyone else's beliefs.

What is a silent meeting?

L: Quakers worship in silence. We come together and spend an hour in silence, and then have coffee or whatever. Quakers are very socially and politically active. They're one of the original peace-keeping churches in the country. So their emphasis tends to be really more on social action.

Which is what you were really doing.

L: Exactly. How can you separate them? So, that was that part of my history.

And you and Sharon?

L: Sharon and I ended our relationship after ten years, and I can't sit here and tell you that it wasn't painful and wasn't difficult. It simply was the thing to do. And it's an example of how you can love each other and grow apart and go in different directions. And there's something that we've done, also, that we think is a little unique. We struggled for a year. We went back and forth for a year. We went to counselors, and we went to mediators, and we did all that good stuff, and we decided that there was something that we wanted—we wanted to be family. And we both wanted that very much. That we had loved each other and did love each other too much to just pack up our toys and go home and end with the anger, the hurt, and the bitterness that most couples end with. So we worked very hard on the relationship, and I'm happy to say that she is my family today, and I am hers. And our lovers may come and go, and we will probably always be the first phone call that we make when we're in trouble or when we're hurting or something.

She is absolutely my dearest friend. We did so many things together during those ten years—the whole coming out process. We marched together in the gay parade every year. You know, we did all that growing and changing together, being politically active and coming out of the closet, you know, making our statements and our stands and seeing the climate change a lot.

What have you seen? What are some of the dominant differences? How is it different today?

L: Well, you know, it might be just simply living in the center of the universe, which is Berkeley, because we live in such an incredibly liberal community that I think there's a danger. I can say, well, look how openly gay you can be, walking down the street with all kinds of buttons and badges and statements, and no one's going to think any different of you. But then, that's probably not true in Wichita.

I think we've come a long, long way in terms of general acceptance. I really do believe that because there's so much education that's gone on. A few people are looking at our lifestyles differently than they did. But then I want to turn right around and say, "However..." We are living in incredibly conservative, right-wing times. Here I am about to say things have changed so much in the last 20 years in terms of being able to be out—there are no circumstances under which I would ever park over a block away from a bar. Never. I will never do that again. I guess I have tasted what it's like to be myself. I have been myself always on the job. That doesn't mean I go to work in the morning with a large signboard that flashes on and off the fact that I am lesbian. But I'm so totally who I am that in about a ten-minute conversation with me, you're going to know. But I guess what I really don't know is how much the world has changed or just how much I have.

Is it that society is more accepting, or is it that we just won't hide anymore?

L: A little of both. I think it's a little of both. One of my favorite writers is Dorothy Parker. I adore Dorothy Parker. I should never even mention her name; you'll be here another three hours.

> "In youth it was a way I had to do my best to please
> And change with every passing lad to suit his theories
> But now I know the things I know and do the things I do
> And if you do not like me so, to hell my love with you."

This is very typical Dorothy Parker, but it also reflects a certain attitude of "I know who I am." And I can go out there, and I think it's self-acceptance probably more than anything else. How do we get people to accept us if we haven't gotten around to doing it ourselves? And I believe that most closeted people—and I know there are some good reasons to be closeted. I'm almost sure there are, somewhere—are closeted because of their self-hatred. Not that they even begin to recognize that. If I go about my life as if it is the most normal thing in the world—which it is—it's real hard for somebody to put something else on you.

Like claiming the word "dyke." At one time it was the worst thing that anyone could say to a woman. I believe that men probably used that word to control their wives, sweethearts, sisters, and lovers for years. If they [the women] showed the slightest assertiveness—"Hey, you're acting like a dyke!" "Oh, my God, don't call me that!" I think you could get them into instant submission calling them a dyke. It's that word.

Now what happens when you say to somebody, "You act just like a dyke." And they say, "You betcha, honey!" I mean, then what? The word didn't work. What happens to all our ugly words when the other person says, "You got it. And don't forget it!" You can do that with nigger, you can do it with kike, spic, gook—all the terrible things human beings call each other. What happens if we turn it around and claim it like the dykes did and said, "That's right buster, and I'm hopping on my little bike and leading the parade!" [*Laughs*] You strip people of their weapons. There isn't a lot that they can hurt you with. Well, I guess that they can fire you and do stuff like that. But I've never been fired. I've never suffered anything bad. There's the little thing at the church. But from the day the lightbulb came on, I was delighted. It was the answer. Everything made sense. Right to today, I've had virtually no negative experiences around being gay or lesbian. None.

alyson books

AFTERGLOW, *edited by Karen Barber.* Filled with the excitement of new love and the remembrances of past ones, *Afterglow* offers well-crafted, imaginative, sexy stories of lesbian desire.

DREAM LOVER, *by Jane Futcher.* The enduring power of adolescent fantasy tempts one woman at an emotional crossroads in later life.

EARLY EMBRACES, *by Lindsey Elder.* Sexily sizzling or softly sensual stories explore the first lesbian experience for women.

THE FEMME MYSTIQUE, *edited by Lesléa Newman. Women's Monthly* says, "Images of so-called 'lipstick lesbians' have become the darlings of the popular media of late. *The Femme Mystique* brings together a broad range of work in which 'real' lesbians who self-identify as femmes speak for themselves about what it means to be femme today."

HEATWAVE: WOMEN IN LOVE AND LUST, *edited by Lucy Jane Bledsoe.* Where can a woman go when she needs a good hot...read? Crawl between the covers of *Heatwave,* a collection of original short stories about women in search of that elusive thing called love.

THE LESBIAN SEX BOOK, *by Wendy Caster.* Informative, entertaining, and attractively illustrated, this handbook is the lesbian sex guide for the '90s. Dealing with lesbian sex practices in a practical, nonjudgmental way, this guide is perfect for the newly out and the eternally curious.

THE PERSISTENT DESIRE, *edited by Joan Nestle.* A generation ago butch-femme identities were taken for granted in the lesbian community. Today, women who think of themselves as butch or femme often face prejudice from both the lesbian community and the straight world. Here, for the first time, dozens of femme and butch lesbians tell their stories of love, survival, and triumph.

PILLOW TALK, *edited by Lesléa Newman.* Climb into bed with this collection of well-crafted, imaginative, and sexy stories: an unbridled celebration of lesbian eroticism. These tales simmer with intrigue, lusty encounters, and lots of hot sex between the sheets as well as some other creative places. These spicy stories will leave you begging for more!

These books and other Alyson titles are available at your local bookstore.
If you can't find a book listed above or would like more information,
please visit our home page on the World Wide Web at **www.alyson.com**.